Polite Society
by
Arthur Devis
1712-1787

Portraits of the
English Country Gentleman
and his Family

Catalogue of the exhibition
The Harris Museum and Art Gallery, Preston, Lancs
October 1st – November 12th 1983

National Portrait Gallery, London
November 25th 1983 – January 29th 1984

An exhibition organised by the Harris Museum and Art Gallery, Preston to commemorate its centenary

with financial assistance from the Arts Council of Great Britain
and
sponsored by the Central Lancashire Development Corporation.

Published by the Harris Museum and Art Gallery, Preston

Design: Primary Colours
Printing: Nelson Brothers Printers Ltd., Chorley

© Harris Museum and Art Gallery, Preston, 1983

ISBN Soft Back   0   9591141   2   X
         Hard back   0   9501141   3   8

Cover illustration: Family in a Garden, 1749. Private Collection (Cat. 28)

FOREWORD

This year the town of Preston celebrates the centenary of the foundation of its municipal art gallery. In 1883 Richard Newsham, a local banker and mill owner, bequeathed his magnificent collection of British paintings to the town on condition that the council undertook to build a gallery for its display. As a result the plans for a Library and Museum, drawn up the year before, were enlarged to comply with Newsham's wishes and the town so acquired an important collection of pictures and an impressive art gallery.

Looking back, this seems to have been a particularly significant and historic event in the town's affairs and it was felt that the occasion of its centenary anniversary should not be allowed to pass without some suitable form of commemoration. The Harris Museum and Art Gallery has chosen to mark this event, therefore, by organising an exhibition devoted to another of its townsmen, the painter, Arthur Devis.

The 'Harris' is extremely pleased that it has been given the valuable support and co-operation of the National Portrait Gallery, thereby securing a London venue for the exhibition, and it must give Prestonians great pleasure that the town is able to share the fruit of its efforts with a much greater number of people and at the same time display its pride on a national stage.

The exhibition, comprising some sixty pictures, is not only the largest ever assembly of the artist's work but the first to have been shown in London. To bring together this impressive number of works would have been impossible without the loan of material from both private and public collections and a special acknowledgement must be made to the owners of pictures, and to the directors and curators of public collections, for their generosity and help.

Perhaps this is an occasion to acknowledge the work of a previous curator at the 'Harris', Sidney Pavière, for it was through his pioneering efforts in the 1930's and his subsequent publication of *The Devis Family of Painters* in 1950 that Arthur Devis was rescued from relative obscurity. Today Devis is rightly regarded as one of the principal innovators of the conversation piece but in Pavière's day few works could cofidently be attributed to him and only Sacheverell Sitwell's *Conversation Pieces: a Survey of English Domestic Portraits and the Painters,* 1936, had previously attempted to unravel the complexities of the genre. In 1980 Ellen G. D'Oench wrote the catalogue for an exhibition held at the Yale Center for British Art further adding to the information that Sidney Pavière had compiled over the years.

Stephen Sartin, Keeper of Fine Art at the Harris Museum and Art Gallery, through his catalogue essay and extensive catalogue notes has added an impressive supplement to this work that has gone before and should be congratulated on the thoroughness and perceptiveness that his writing reveals. He has been able through his research to unravel much of the obscurity of Devis' origins and to build up a much clearer picture of the artist's patrons and associates. He has also investigated the myths and realities of Devis' depiction of the English country gentleman, which suggest that the artist, generally regarded as an accurate chronicler of social life, was often describing not so much his provincial sitters' way of living but rather their aspiration to metropolitan fashion.

Mr. Sartin in his acknowledgements refers to all of the people who have helped in various ways to make the exhibition a success, but a special debt of gratitude is owed to the Arts Council of Great Britain and to the Central Lancashire

Development Corporation who have each provided indispensible financial support. I should also like to record my thanks to Dr. Hayes of the National Portrait Gallery for giving advice and assistance and for writing the catalogue introduction.

It is sincerely hoped that the exhibition affords pleasure and stimulation to its visitors and that as a result they may be able to join in this our centenary anniversary celebration.

Michael Cross,
Curator,
Harris Museum and Art Gallery, Preston.

ACKNOWLEDGEMENTS

Many people have assisted in the preparation of this exhibition, and I should like to express my gratitude to the directors and staff of the museums and art galleries I have visited, and also to the many private individuals who provided me with much useful information.

I wish to record my particular thanks to my colleague Michael Cross, curator of the Harris Museum and Art Gallery. To him must be given the credit for suggesting the exhibition in the first place. He has also undertaken the arduous and time-consuming task of organising the exhibition and editing the catalogue.

I am grateful to Mrs. C. Williams, Lancashire Records Office; R. G. A. Chesterman, Cheshire Records Office; Terence Shaw and Ann Dennison, Preston Central Reference Library; Brian Hawkes, Preston Borough Council; Simon Cotton, who has also lent two paintings to the exhibition; Col. D. A. S. Houghton; Paul Monod; Lady Damaris Stewart; Kay Staniland and Dilys Blum, London Museum; G. Hughes-Hartman; L. W. Neary; John Ayre; Elizabeth Einberg, Tate Gallery; Sarah Wimbush, National Portrait Gallery; Dr. D. G. C. Allan, Royal Society of Arts; Mike Sixsmith, Arts Council of Great Britain; and the staff of the Witt Library.

I also wish to express my acknowledgement to Ellen G. D'Oench, whose researches, which led to the exhibition *The Conversation Piece: Arthur Devis and His Contemporaries* held at the Yale Center for British Art in 1980, added much to present knowledge of Arthur Devis and his work.

However, the success of an exhibition ultimately depends on the willingness of owners to lend important works in their possession, and in this context I am much indebted to Duncan Robinson, Yale Center for British Art, New Haven; Alan Shestack, Yale University Art Gallery, New Haven; Dr. John Hayes and the Trustees of the National Portrait Gallery; Alan Bowness and the Trustees of the Tate Gallery; Elizabeth Conran, Bowes Museum, Barnard Castle; Edith Tyson, Lancaster City Museum; Trustees of the Museum of the King's Own Royal Regiment, Lancaster; Mrs. R. M. Paisey, Leicestershire County Council, Museums and Art Galleries; Louise Mary West, Ferens Art Gallery, Hull; Dr. C. M. Kauffmann, Victoria and Albert Museum; Timothy Stevens, Walker Art Gallery, Liverpool; the Trustees of R. J. Meade-Fetherstonhaugh, dec'd.; Capt P. J. B. Drury-Lowe; Mrs. William Dalison Keown-Boyd; Roger Fleetwood Hesketh; Mr. Fitzroy Newdigate; St. John Gore, the National Trust; David Posnett, Leger Galleries; the Trustees of the Marchioness of Downshire Settlement; Mrs. S. Foulkes, Metropolitan Borough of Wigan, Department of Leisure; and the many private owners who wish to remain anonymous.

For technical assistance thanks are also due to Joan Delve, North Western Museum and Art Gallery Service; and Wyn and Craig Smith, Norwyn Photographics, Preston.

Finally, I should like to express my appreciation to Audrey Maxwell and Carol Smith of the Harris staff for their shouldering of extra administrative and clerical duties which the preparation of the exhibition has entailed, and also to Jacquie Meredith, Paula Iley, and the staff of the National Portrait Gallery for their enthusiastic support.

Stephen V. Sartin,
Keeper of Fine Art,
Harris Museum and Art Gallery

Introduction

Dr. John Hayes,
Director,
National Portrait Gallery,
London

INTRODUCTION

Arthur Devis was one of the few better known British painters of the eighteenth century who devoted himself almost exclusively to a single genre of painting. Richard Wilson, the great landscape painter, who originally had been a portraitist but then abandoned the easier profits of this practice, was another. Most artists, if not actively seeking variety, like Hogarth or John Hamilton Mortimer, had more than one string to their bow. Devis's specialism was the informal small-scale portrait in domestic surroundings, the figures in his groups disposed in an easy familiarity which accounted for the name given by contemporaries (and retained by art and social historians) to this popular genre: the conversation piece. Because the genre *was* popular, some explanation is required for the fact that Devis, who for twenty years carried on a successful practice from a studio in a fashionable part of London, Great Queen Street, was eclipsed by the 1760's (when he was only in his fifties), scarcely noticed at his death in 1787, and totally forgotten thereafter until the revival of interest in Georgian life and manners in the period between the wars. By focussing our attention on this problem we may learn something about the nature both of portraiture and of patronage in eighteenth-century England.

Perhaps we should begin our investigation by analysing in some detail the characteristics of Devis' style. Let us take for example the group of John Bacon and his family (Cat. No. 10). painted in about 1742–3, shortly after Devis settled permanently in London. This picture, which includes six figures, is about two and a half feet high by just over four feet long. The first impression is of life in miniature; and this is reinforced by the meticulous technique. All the components of the picture – the features of the sitters, the costume, the carpet and other furnishings, the scientific instruments – are delineated (and delineated rather than modelled, though it is true that Devis gives his heads a broad, eggshell-like rotundity) with an obvious concern for verisimilitude; Devis had an immense sensitivity to materials, especially fabrics. The crisp outlining of the figures gives them a stiff, somewhat doll-like appearance, and it will come as no surprise to learn that, in common with other artists of the period, Devis possessed a small mannequin, with its own (still extant) wardrobe of clothes, upon which he depended for the painting of the human figure. The figures in this conversation are informally disposed in three distinct groups – any one of which could have formed a portrait subject in its own right – tied together by a loose but effective compositional rhythm. Further, they are all comfortably at leisure after the day's activity, which contributes to the domestic flavour. John Bacon is holding forth to his son, who has a flute and some music in his hands, and does so with a pointed and elegant gesture; though the boy is listening intently to his father's words, however, the latter's discourse lacks animation, since, as so often with Devis, the two figures are visually unrelated, and John Bacon, as a result, appears all the more stilted and puppet-like. The group of mother and daughter, and the two children building cards, are more successfully managed. The figures are set in a fashionably appointed, if somewhat bare, interior; there is a fine and colourful Turkey carpet, and, over the mantelpiece, appropriate Dutch seventeenth-century decorative pictures, a landscape and a seaport respectively. A quadrant, a telescope and other instruments reflect Bacon's scientific interests – he was elected a Fellow of the Royal Society in 1750 – and the grisaille portrait roundels of worthies (Sir Francis Bacon, Milton, Newton and Pope) his pretensions to learning; these, however, are props like the cannon in a Reynolds portrait of a distinguished general, and there is nothing about the room, in spite of the meticulous observation and rendering of detail, which really convinces one that it is an actual interior, the home of the Bacons, as opposed to an idealised setting devised to reflect their position in the world — indeed Devis is believed to have painted only one identifiable interior, the Gothic library in the portrait of Sir Roger Newdigate (Cat. No. 38). The curtain on the right, evidently introduced for compositional reasons, since it bears no relation to an actual window in the room, hovers over the scene and completes the impression of an artificial and contrived space, a stage set, in fact, upon which the curtain will eventually fall. Similarly, in Devis's groups posed outdoors, the landscape settings are very often generalised impressions of a particular countryside, appropriate, if delicately rendered, backdrops to the figure composition. Joseph Burke, in his *Oxford History*, has deftly characterised Devis's 'essentially . . . doll's-house world . . . .. His interiors have the rectilinear neatness and dovetailing precision of the model cabinet-maker's masterwork; his landscapes could be cut out for a toy theatre; and his silhouette figures positively invite the scissors.' Yet herein, in the very fragility of Devis's world and Devis's human automata, lies the distinctive appeal of his art.

The verisimilitude of detail, if not of setting, in Devis's portraits, the accurate, painstaking representation of costume and furnishings which makes his work such a joy to the twentieth-century spectator, and especially to the student of the Georgian age, placed him low down the scale as a painter in his own time. For, in common with the realism of Stubbs, a painter similarly unnoticed at his death and similarly forgotten by subsequent generations, his work was not in conformity with academic theory, as codified in the seventeenth century. 'We are sure,' observed Sir Joshua Reynolds, 'that it is expressing the general effect of the whole which alone can give to objects their true . . . character . . . when the general effect only is presented to us by a skilful hand, it appears to express the object represented in a more lively manner than the minutest resemblance would do.' For Reynolds — and his influence was paramount in the second half of the eighteenth century, both as the most highly paid portrait painter of his age and as the first President of the Royal Academy — portraiture had to be idealized, not seeking to explore the idiosyncrasies of individual physiognomy, but elevating likeness to an expression of character and of type; in some of his own work he even employed generalised drapery rather than contemporary fashionable dress so that his pictures would not date as the years went by but appear timeless, like the classical sculpture he so deeply admired. Only by these means could portraiture, comparatively low in the academic hierarchy of genres which was headed by history painting — the representation of noble actions preferably from the Bible or classical literature — approach the level of high art.

Devis's portraiture was definitely not high art. Yet he did in his own way subscribe to current academic theory through including in his portrait of the Bacon family the attributes of the man of science, thus elevating the sitter to the company of Newton, and by the very act of not painting an actual room in the Bacons' London or country house — something which would otherwise seem very strange to us and which we would certainly regard as extraordinary in a present-day painter of family groups. Moreover, in the mid and later 1750's, following Reynolds's almost immediate success in London after his fruitful years of study in Italy — the latter's mighty full-length of Commodore Keppel, dating from 1753-4, with its noble expression, commanding stride, stormy generalised background and bold chiaroscuro, was intended to be, and is, a milestone in

British portraiture — Devis consciously aimed at producing more impressive figures and at achieving greater psychological subtlety. *Mr and Mrs Edward Parker* (Cat. No. 42) and *Alicia and Jane Clarke* (Cat. No. 45), set against landscape backgrounds the sensitivity of which may owe something to a sight of early Gainsborough, though the style is that of George Smith of Chichester, are excellent examples of this phase, and his portrait of Assheton Curzon with his tutor, Dr. Roger Mather, painted about 1754–5 (Cat. No. 34), a work of exceptional interest. For here the figures, elegantly postured as always in Devis, are related to each other as convincingly as John Bacon and his son are not: the tutor is discussing, perhaps translating, a passage in the book he is holding and the youth is carefully attentive to what he is saying. The figures are also larger in scale than was customary with Devis, while the heads and the tutor's demonstrative left hand stand out as the focal points of the picture against the darks of clothes and background in the way we associate with, for example, Reynolds's masterly portrait of Laurence Sterne; moreover, there is for once a complete absence of clutter in the room. But, in making the comparison with Reynolds, one must also remark Devis's characteristic lack, in the highlights, of the softness, texture and variety in the play of light we find in Reynolds. And it is precisely Devis's linearism and lack of differentiation in modelling which, however much he might modify his overall approach to portraiture — and increasingly he found this difficult — prevented his finding favour in the new age. The heir to his long success in his chosen genre was an equally meticulous but broader and more sophisticated painter, and one who was to enjoy considerable royal patronage, Johann Zoffany (Fig. I).

Fig I   Johann Zoffany. John, 3rd Duke of Atholl, with his family, beside the Tay at Dunkeld. 1765–7.   Canvas, 36¾ × 62¼ inches. The Duke of Atholl.

11

In 1765, the date of one of Zoffany's most charming portraits of the royal children in an interior at Buckingham House, Lord John Cavendish wrote of a projected portrait of his nephew, William, fifth Duke of Devonshire, to be painted by Devis for the duke's tutor: 'I am much afraid it will be frightful for I understand, his pictures are all of a sort; they are whole lengths of about two feet long; & the person is always represented in a genteel attitude, either leaning against a pillar, or standing by a flower pot, or leading an Italian greyhound in a string, or in some other such ingenious posture.' The irony is that, forty years earlier, such pictures would not only have been fashionable, even among dukes, but advanced in style. The informality of Devis's portraiture contrasted sharply with the baroque conventions that had been handed down from the time of Van Dyck and which still dominated British portraiture in the age of Kneller. Devis was not himself an innovator. But he sprang from a more prosaic tradition in portraiture than that propagated by Kneller, and had the good fortune to be swept along in the wake of one of the most remarkable innovative movements in the history of British art, a movement which in part reflected the influence of the French rococo and in part the aspirations and cast of mind of a lively middle-class public for literature, theatre and the visual arts.

The informal tradition in British portraiture was an offshoot of a specific kind of topography. Prospects of the countryside, pictures which illustrated the varied cultivation of the land and the prosperity that ensued, were the most popular form of landscape painting in seventeenth-century Britain, and from this genre developed the country house portrait, typically a bird's-eye view of an estate with its focus the great house. Wealthy landowners of the period were as concerned to record their houses, often newly built, and the surrounding gardens, land, domestic and rural activities as they were to have themselves and their families portrayed, and in 1707 a volume of engravings after Leonard Knyff's prospects of great houses was published as *Britannia Illustrata*. The whole point of such scenes, if ultimately vanity, was record: topographical accuracy and particularity. Now, germane to our theme, sometimes, and increasingly frequently in the early eighteenth century, hunting or hawking scenes, or informal portrait groups, were included in these pictures, perched upon an eminence in the foreground; Charles I and Henrietta Maria, with a number of their courtiers, were portrayed exactly in this manner, high above Greenwich, by Jan van Belcamp and Adrian van Stalbemt. One of the last purveyors of the country house prospect with such foreground portraiture was Peter Tillemans, a Flemish artist working in England who was principally a sporting painter, and it was in his studio, for several years before his death in 1734, that Devis is supposed to have commenced his career. The portrait of Thomas Lister and his family in the Art Institute of Chicago, painted about 1740-1, derives from Tillemans in its arrangement, though the scale of the figures is closer to Wootton's practice and contains in embryo much that was soon to become characteristic of Devis's own style. Two gentlemen are standing on the left, one of them with his hand tucked inside his waistcoat in the manner approved by contemporary books of etiquette, the other pointing towards the huntsmen on the right of the canvas; between them are two young girls with a doe. The landscape beyond, and falling away behind, is very much in the nature of a backdrop, but includes some of the breed of white cattle for which the estate was famous, and, in the distance, a view of Gisburne Park, which Lister had rebuilt in the 1720's in an austere Palladian style.

The country house portrait played a significant part in the development of the conversation piece. But it was not the only influence. Family groups posed informally, replete with domestic incidents and pet animals, seen either indoors or outdoors, as exemplified by Metsu and de Hooch respectively, were as popular in bourgeois Holland of the seventeenth century as the grand formal group portraits of guildsmen or militiamen we associate with Frans Hals and of which the best known is surely Rembrandt's *The Night Watch*. Nonetheless, in spite of the many, admittedly minor, Dutch artists who settled or worked in England in the seventeenth century, the influence of such groups on British portraiture is hard to trace; patronage in this country was still largely aristocratic, and the example of the court painters, Lely and Kneller, thus all-pervasive. It is more the 'drolls' of Brouwer or Teniers, which the early eighteenth-century English art chroniclers, Benjamin Buckeridge and George Vertue, described as conversations, that were taken up, largely through the agency of Egbert van Heemskerk, active in England from the 1670's until his death in 1704. According to Vertue, his pictures were much 'in vogue among waggish Collectors, & the lower Rank of Virtuosi;' one such 'waggish Collector' may have been Richard, fifth Earl of Dorset, as a small tavern scene by Heemskerk, signed and dated 1675, is at Knole. An unusual English portrait group of the 1720's derived from Dutch scenes of low life is the painting in the same collection entitled *The Steward's Room at Knole*, by John van der Gucht, in which the family retainers are depicted off duty, smoking and drinking. Hogarth's *A Midnight Modern Conversation*, a scene of drunken stupor in which the figures are not, however, intended to be portraits, derives from the same source but is more satirical in intent than Dutch painting of similar subjects.

There is little doubt that, as Joseph Burke has pointed out, the conversation piece had its roots in genre; that is, subject painting of one kind or another which had no pretension to high art or aristocratic favour. Dutch genre was one factor in its growth. But the chief was the art of the French rococo, an aesthetic in which diminutive forms and gaiety of colour were significant elements. Watteau himself, the most ravishing painter of his age, was in London briefly in 1719-20, to consult Dr Richard Mead, the celebrated physician who was also a great art lover and collector, and the two pictures he painted for him at that time, *L'Amour Paisible* and *Comédiens Italiens*, must have been well known, since Mead's gallery was open to visitors. Then, in the mid 1720's, a follower of Watteau, Philip Mercier, came to settle in England; it seems to have been Mercier, and to a lesser extent Robert Tournières, who translated the fêtes galantes and fancy compositions of Watteau into terms of portraiture – though Watteau had already led the way with such engaging fantasies as his self-portrait with his friend Julienne playing the 'cello, engraved in 1727 – and it was certainly Mercier who created in England the related genres of the conversation piece and the small-scale portrait with landscape setting. The master of the one was Hogarth and of the other the young Gainsborough.

Mercier's delightful group of Lord Tyrconnel and his family with Belton House seen in the distance, painted in about 1725-6 (Fig. II), which is entirely Watteauesque in its handling, figure types and semi-arcadian background, and incorporates for good measure the favourite rococo subject of the swing, may lay fair claim to be the earliest English conversation piece of the kind that was to become familiar in succeeding decades. In 1728-9 Mercier was appointed official painter to Frederick, Prince of Wales, a cultivated connoisseur and patron whose sympathies lay with a more informal kind of art than prevailed, and whose active encouragement and understanding of the younger artists and craftsmen associated with the English rococo, as it developed, cannot be over-estimated. The group which Mercier painted in 1733 of the Prince and his sisters performing music in the gardens of Kew Palace is a revolutionary portrait of royal sitters, depicting them at their ease in a favourite occupation, wholly without pretensions or idealisation.

Fig II   Philip Mercier. John, 1st Viscount Tyrconnel with his family, at Belton House. 1725–6.   Canvas, 25½ × 29¾ inches. Executors of the late Lord Brownlow.

Conversation pieces and small-scale portraits seem to have become fashionable overnight, first perhaps as novelties more than anything else; in 1731 Vertue described Charles Philips, the neighbour of Devis, as having 'met with great encouragement amongst People of fashion – even some of ye Royal Family,' and, during the 1730's, grandees and their families sat to specialists in the genre such as Gawen Hamilton, Philips and other lesser-known painters of whom Henesy, who in 1737 painted Baptist, fourth Earl of Gainsborough and his daughters, is one. It is not known how these aristocratic connoisseurs related conversations to portraiture in the grand manner, but presumably in the same way as they bought Dutch genre no less enthusiastically than the academically more acceptable works of Claude or Guido Reni.

By 1740, however, the vogue had slipped in the social scale, though nearly a decade later we still find Devis painting Peregrine Bertie, third Duke of Ancaster, a patron of Hogarth, with his brothers and sisters. It was Hogarth, the most versatile and influential English artist of the second quarter of the eighteenth century, and the central figure in the English rococo, who did most to popularise the conversation piece. As Vertue noted in 1730: 'The daily success of Mr Hogarth in painting small family peices & Conversations with so much Air and agreeableness Causes him to be much followed, & esteemd whereby he has much imployment & like to be a master of great reputation in that way' (Fig. III).

Fig III   William Hogarth. William Wollaston with his wife and relatives, probably at his house in St. James's Square. 1730.   Canvas, 39 × 49 inches. Executors of the late H. C. Wollaston.

Hogarth's range, if calculated, yet remained phenomenal. In addition to informal family groups outdoors and indoors (the limit of Devis's inventive powers), he painted complex assemblies in the tradition of Marcellus Laroon's levées or musical parties, weddings, amateur theatricals, groups in a ship's cabin, individuals in the privacy of the bedroom, babies in their cradles. He overflowed into reportage with his group of a committee of the House of Commons interrogating the governor of the Fleet Prison, and with his portrait of the notorious murderess, Sarah Malcolm, based on a sketch he made during a visit to her in prison. Moving away from the portrayal of individuals to the representation of types, which was his main preoccupation, he painted theatrical scenes, notably from *The Beggar's Opera*, and composed genre subjects with moral implications, rich in allusive detail, of which the most celebrated are his series of moral tales, *A Harlot's Progress, A Rake's Progress* and *Marriage à la Mode*. All were executed with a marvellous feeling for compositional flow and rhythm, and a sensuous handling of paint, sparkling in its surface glitter, characteristic of the rococo style. Perhaps only in *The Swaine Family* (Cat. No. 30) does Devis approach a genuine rococo rhythm in his figure grouping.

Many of Hogarth's conversations, and all his modern moral subjects, were engraved. This was an essential part of his purpose, for by this means they reached a wide audience. In the decades following the Revolution Settlement of 1688, business, commerce and enterprise flourished as never before and a new and prosperous middle class, whose ideals were the bourgeois ones of hard work, thrift, piety, social conformity and a sense of order, came into being; it was to this new public, eager for education and instruction, that Addison addressed *The Spectator*, Defoe his narratives, Richardson his novels and Hogarth his engravings. There was a demand for the literal, the domestic, the improving and the moral. Breeding, etiquette, good manners, decorum, in short the social graces applauded and enumerated by Fielding and Lord Chesterfield, were regarded as the foundation of civilised society and conduct. 'Much variety & correctnes of mode & manner of the time & habits:' so Vertue characterised the work of Gawen Hamilton. The figures in Batholomew Dandridge's conversation pieces, of which *The Price Family*, dating from about 1728-30, is the most elaborate, are essays in the art of deportment, and it was Dandridge who was commissioned to execute the designs for the postures in François Nivelon's well-known manual, *The Rudiments of Genteel Behaviour*, published in 1737.

Many of Devis's postures and gestures closely reflect those in Nivelon's treatise, and it is clear, as one surveys his work, that the costume, furniture, arrangement of porcelain on a mantelpiece, children's kites, decorative paintings and architectural features, follow current fashions of which the bourgeois and landowning patrons who commissioned conversations from him appear inordinately proud. Nothing is allowed to disturb the even tenor of Devis's world. Nowhere do we find the ruffled carpets which enliven a Hogarth or a Gawen Hamilton interior. No-one is actually pouring water into a teapot, as the butler is doing in Hogarth's *The Strode Family*, let alone upsetting the table, like the dog in the same artist's *A Children's Party*. The emphasis is on possessions, gentility and status, rather than upon any kind of action; even in the mid 1750's when, as we have seen, he was becoming aware of the challenge of a new generation of painters, a scene in which the attention of the figures is focussed upon a dead pheasant rather incongruously brought into a room by a young sportsman is the furthest which Devis will allow himself to go. As soon as the postures and fashions of the second quarter of the eighteenth century became obsolete, Devis became obsolete, too. In the 1760's Zoffany effectively supplanted him. It was Zoffany who succeeded to the mantle of Hogarth in his naturalness, his animation, his capacity for narrative, and his ability to enlarge the scope of the conversation piece and of domestic portraiture with fresh subject-matter. With his *Tribuna in the Uffizi*, exhibited at the Royal Academy in 1780, we are in a complex and sophisticated new world.

John Hayes

Arthur Devis : His Life and Art

Stephen V. Sartin,
Keeper of Fine Art,
Harris Museum and Art Gallery,
Preston

ARTHUR DEVIS: HIS LIFE AND ART

Arthur Devis was born at Preston in Lancashire on February 12, 1712. He was the son of Anthony Devis of Cockerham on the north west coast, and Ellen Rauthmell (or Rothmell), sister of Richard Rauthmell of Whitewell, Bowland.[1] From the comparatively few records which exist it is known that his father, Anthony, was apprenticed to a local cabinet maker about the year 1701.[2] When Arthur was born the family was living in Church Street at a house and joiner's shop on a site now occupied by the Red Lion public house, opposite the Parish Church.[3] It is interesting that in those early years the town scriveners always wrote the family name as 'Davis' or 'Davies' and continued to do so until 1720.[4]

In November 1714 Anthony Devis was elected a Free-Inn-Burgess (or freeman) of Preston. This was the first stage in realising his ambition to hold high political office in the town, the consequences of which had so important an influence on the artistic patronage which his son, Arthur, was to gain in later years.

Arthur Devis left Preston some time between 1722 and 1728.[5] It is probable that through the artist, Hamlet Winstanley, he had been introduced to the Flemish topographical and sporting painter, Peter Tillemans, who was working for the Earl of Derby at Knowsley Hall, near Liverpool, some time before 1729.[6] Winstanley must certainly have been known to Anthony Devis because he had painted several commissions in Preston in the 1720s – in particular, in 1721, a portrait of Sir Edward Stanley, who himself succeeded to the Derby title, and who lived at Patten House, Church Street, several hundred yards from the Devis household.

Little is known of Arthur Devis' associations with Peter Tillemans, but there can be no doubt that he worked for him. Edward Edwards, who must have known Devis, describes him as having been "the pupil of Peter Tilemans."[7] There is also the evidence of the catalogue of the sale of the contents of Tillemans' studio, held in April 1733 prior to his retirement due to ill health. Devis' name appears in seven lots, as having painted various landscapes after Marco (Ricci), G. P. Pannini, and Van Bloom (Jan van Bloemen).[8] It is significant that the very artists whom he copied in these early years, although admittedly popular at the time, are the ones whose works appear most frequently in his paintings of interiors in later years. Tangible evidence that he not only worked for Tillemans, but also closely followed his style on occasions, can be gained from comparing his painting of *Hoghton Tower from Duxon Hill, Lancashire* (Cat. 3) with that by his master of *Uppark, West Sussex* (Cat. 4). It is surely unlikely that Devis, who worked for Tillemans and possessed such a facility for imitating his work, should only have executed the one painting in a similar manner, and it makes possible his authorship of some works doubtfully attributed to his master.

The retirement of Tillemans in 1733 marks the end of the first phase of the career of Devis, in which his training had specifically been in landscape painting. After a visit to Preston in 1734 and 1735, during which time he painted *Hoghton Tower from Duxon Hill, Lancashire,* he once more returned to London, where, with an uncertain career before him, he decided that financial success lay not with landscape painting but with portraiture. This was a courageous decision to make for someone who had not received any training in portrait painting. He set up a studio in Great Queen Street, Lincoln's Inn Fields, an area with a flourishing artists' community, and adopted the fashionable form of portrait painting of the day – the conversation piece.

19

The origin of the conversation piece can clearly be seen in seventeenth-century Dutch genre paintings, in which characters are placed in the intimate surroundings of every-day life. Artists in eighteenth-century London adapted the idea to their own purposes, by transforming the nameless figures into portraits of actual people and transporting them from their own tavern or courtyard to the Georgian house or its surrounding landscape garden. In addition, the English artists, who were temperamentally suited to the Dutch tradition of adhering to nature as closely as possible, attempted to record every featre in the painting with the same verisimilitude, regardless of its importance, and to capture with painstaking skill textural qualities such as the shimmer of light on a silk or satin costume, the glazed surface of a pot, the polished wood of a musical instrument, or metal fire-irons in a grate. Perhaps where they failed, with the probable exception of William Hogarth, was in being able to capture the dramatic rapport and the convincing inter-relationship between one person and another in their compositions, such as one always finds, even in the lesser Dutch masters. Invariably, in the English conversation piece, the association of one figure with another is by a simple gesture — thus a gentleman declares his heir simply by pointing towards him, a wife declares her love for her husband by presenting him with a piece of honeysuckle, or a husband might tell his family of a commission he has received by holding a letter before them. Apart from this minimal communication, each figure remains frozen within him- or herself, remote from the other participants in the anecdote.

However, if on the whole the English conversation piece lacked animation, it possessed a sophisticated politeness and an elegant charm that was derived from paintings, engravings, and tapestries by and after Antoine Watteau, and popularised by his fellow-countrymen, Andien de Clermont, Philip Mercier, and Hubert Gravelot, all of whom had settled in London in the early years of the eighteenth century. The influence of Gravelot was twofold — from the mid 1730s to 1740s he collaborated with Francis Hayman in executing the decorative paintings for Vauxhall Gardens, thereby introducing the grace of French rococo art to London society; and, being the principal illustrator in the capital at the time, he was chosen, again with Hayman, to design and engrave the plates for the first illustrated edition of Samuel Richardson's novel, *Pamela*.[9] The narrative of this immensely popular work unfolds as a series of letters to and from Pamela Andrews, a young maidservant, and describes at length her master's attempts to seduce her, and her virtue in resisting his designs. A second section concerns her marriage to him, his profligacy, and their ultimate happiness in family life. Interestingly, Richardson's method often is to write an episode as if he is seeing it as a conversation piece. A good example of this is Pamela's description (letter 61) of a scene in the nursery, which Gravelot can have had little difficulty in illustrating (Fig. IV) —

"THEN, Madam, we all proceed hand-in-hand together to the Nursery, to my *Charley* and *Jemmy*; And in this happy Retirement, so much my Delight in the Absence of my best Beloved, imagine you see me seated, surrounded with the Joy and the Hope of my future Prospects, as well as my present Comforts. MISS *Goodwin* imagine you see, on my Right-hand, sitting on a Velvet Stool, because she is eldest, and a Miss: *Billy* on my Left, in a little Cane Elbow-Chair, because he is eldest, and a good Boy: My *Davers*, and my sparkling eyd *Pamela*, with my *Charley* between them, on little silken Cushions at my Feet, hand-in-hand, their pleased Eyes looking up to my more delighted ones, and my sweet-natur'd promising *Jemmy* in my Lap; the Nurses and the Cradle just behind us, and the Nursery Maids delightedly pursuing some useful Needlework, for the dear Charmers of my Heart — All as hush and as still, as Silence itself, as the pretty Creatures generally are, when their little watchful Eyes see my Lips beginning to open: For they take great notice already, of my Rule of Two Ears to One Tongue, insomuch that if *Billy* or *Davers* are either of them breaking the Mum, as they call it, they are immediately hush, at any time, if I put my Finger to my Lip, or if Miss points hers to her Ears, even to the breaking of a Word in two, as it were: And yet all my Boys are as lively as so many Birds; while my *Pamela* is chearful, easy, soft, gentle, always smiling, but modest and harmless as a Dove."

The above passage suggests that, although the conversation piece had developed as a genre before Richardson put pen to paper, its form makes it peculiarly suited to the introduction of a narrative which must have been at least partially responsible for its adoption in England in the first place. Not surprisingly, in addition to Gravelot and Hayman, other artists were inspired by episodes in *Pamela*, Joseph Highmore executed a series of twelve pictures based on its principal events, and Philip Mercier added a French licentiousness to Pamela's character by painting her with bosom and right thigh bared, drawing back the curtain of her bed.[10]

A factor which must have encouraged Devis to become a painter of conversation pieces and of small whole-length portraits was the greater flexibility such a genre of paintings allowed him by comparison with straightforward

Fig V   J. F. Nollekens, Two Children Playing, c. 1740. Private Collection

Fig IV   Hubert Gravelot, Pamela with her Children in the Nursery. Engraved illustration to Richardson's *'Pamela'*, 3rd edit., 1742, vol. IV, p.475, Private Collection.

portraiture. His early self-portrait (Cat. 1) which dates from about 1737 has, one senses, been painted as a justification of his faith in his newly-found vocation. However, it betrays a flatness of form and a lack of awareness of the possibilities of the use of light and shadow to place the figure in space, which one would expect in someone lacking studio training in the subject. The features of the face have been carefully delineated, capturing the textural qualities of eyes, nose and lips with a respect for detail reminiscent of a Flemish painting; but in concentrating on this aspect Devis has lost the spatial relationship of one eye to the other, or of the nose to the cheek immediately behind it, or indeed the sculptural form of the head. In effect it is a flat design coincident with the surface plane of the canvas. The rest of the figure not only lacks a sense of underlying anatomical structure beneath the coat, but also appears to be insensitively drawn by comparison with the face. The same may be said of Devis' other full-scale portraits, with the exceptions of his self-portrait (Cat. 33) painted circa 1754, when a new dramatic approach briefly reduced his dependence on careful rendering of fine detail, and his life-size whole-length portrait of Nicholas Fazackerley (Cat. 52), unique in his work, in which the figure and its surroundings are conceived as an enlarged version of one of his small whole-length portraits.

By comparison, a facility in painting a conversation piece depended less on capturing a perfect representation of the physiognomy of the sitters, which on a large scale would present problems of investing them with a living character beyond the scope of Devis' technique, and more on placing them in the context of their surroundings, or more importantly in those to which they had aspirations. It was, in a sense, an easier option for Devis, who was able to reduce the scale of the sitter to manageable proportions, to invest him or her with more generalised features, which would be more than compensated for by graceful deportment, and to recreate a miniature world of clear-cut architectural forms, sumptuous costumes, delicate fabrics and furnishings, exquisite still-lifes of work baskets, houses made of cards, and scientific instruments, all brought together with a verisimilitude which would almost deceive the sitters into believing that they actually existed and belonged to them. Certainly there is a degree of dissimulation in the paintings of Devis which was a conceit perfectly well understood and accepted by whoever commissioned them at the time, but which, over the two centuries since they were painted, has been forgotten. This has important implications when it is considered that Devis' paintings, among others, are used to illustrate eighteenth-century life, and often carry misleading titles which suggest that the persons portrayed in them are in familiar surroundings. There are, of course, paintings in which Devis is accurately representing a particular topographical view or, much more rarely, a known interior. Sir Roger Newdigate (Cat. 38) is specifically shown in his "gothick" library at Arbury Hall, the drawing for which may well have been supplied by Sir Roger himself; and in the painting of Col. John Sabine and his family (Cat. 44) there is a prospect of Tewin House, Hertfordshire (demolished 1807), with its nearby church which still survives. On the other hand, whilst few would be deceived by Devis' representation of Dr. Clayton's school in Salford (Cat. 9) which in reality was an unprepossessing brick building, it could well be imagined that Robert Dashwood and his wife, Anne (Cat. 18), lived in the house which is represented in the painting. This, however, was not so. Devis painted an identical interior into which he introduced the figures of Mr. and Mrs. Richard Bull, who lived at Ongar in Essex.

Devis also extended his magical world of make-believe to the sitters themselves, investing them with all the social graces of polite society. Personal idiosyncracies which they may have possessed, and which do so much to determine individual character, were suppressed and in their place were substituted a genteel attitude and elegant deportment thought proper for persons of 'good breeding.' For his standard Devis could draw on several sources which were available to him at the time, in particular François Nivelon's manual of deportment, *Rudiments of Genteel Behaviour,* published in London in 1737. This volume, which comprises twelve engraved illustrations by Louis-Philip Boitard after Bartholomew Dandridge, certainly could have been the source which Devis used for the attitudes of figures in several of his paintings – one of the engraved illustrations is a mirror image of the pose taken up by Nicholas Fazackerley (Cat. 52), while another comes close to the portrait of Barbara, wife of Edward Parker, of Browsholme Hall, near Clitheroe (Cat. 42). Devis must also have been familiar with the numerous engravings after Watteau published in London and Paris, which included his *Figures de modes* and *Figures françois* published in London in 1728 under the title *A Drawing Book of Figures.* Watteau's disciple, Philip Mercier, has already been mentioned as having been one of several French artists who made a significant contribution to the development of the English conversation piece, and indeed his painting of *Lord Tyrconnel and his Family* must be one of the earliest examples of the genre in England. However, any influence he may have had on Devis is limited more to the familiar domestic scenes found in his paintings and engravings rather that the sentimental way in which he expresses them. Something of Mercier can be seen in the child building a house of cards in Devis' painting, *Children in an Interior* (Cat. 12). There is even a sense of the fleeting moment, unusual in his work, in which the child appears momentarily distracted by the spectator. As for the other children present, the young boy who should be playing with the kite stands there almost oblivious to its existence, while the child astride a hobby-horse appears immobile and silent. It is interesting to compare Devis' treatment of the subject with a painting, *Two Children Playing* (Fig. V), by J. F. Nollekens, which must have been inspired by the works of Philip Mercier. These children are animated, and the house of cards is in a state of collapse with cards falling to the floor. Nevertheless, the meticulous technique of Devis, in which even the children themselves become part of an exquisite still-life, enables him to create a perception of tangible reality which in some respects is more convincing than comparable works by more spontaneous artists.

It was a common practice for Devis' fellow artists to make use of the lay-figure (See Cat. 55 and Fig. VI). This was a large doll, with its own wardrobe of clothes, constructed with cleverly-articulating joints to enable it as closely as possible to take up the attitudes of a living person. Such lay-figures, although found in most academies of drawing, were by no means confined in their use to students; they were owned by some of the most eminent artists of the time, among whom were Sir Joshua Reynolds and Thomas Gainsborough. Generally the lay-figure was regarded as a substitute for the sitter when he was not in the studio, but it was also employed to help the artist in constructing his compositions, particularly in the case of the conversation piece, by enabling him to determine suitable attitudes and correct lighting for the figures. However, no lay-figure could convincingly imitate the subtle and relaxed poses of a living person, and the importance of drawing from life was regarded as an essential part of an artist's

Fig VI   Artist's Lay-Figure, formerly owned by Louis-François Roubiliac, c. 1740.
The Museum of London, (Cat. 55)

training. It is significant that in later years one of the first resolutions of the Council of the Royal Academy was to provide for regular life classes for its students.

Perhaps because of his lack of training in life-drawing, Devis placed great reliance on the use of the lay-figure. In this he was by no means alone — the paintings of several of his contemporaries show that it played a significant part in their studio practice. However, in Devis' hands it became a new vehicle for expression in which he deliberately exploited its doll-like characteristics. There is, of course, an element of this in the delicate grace of most representations of the human figure in rococo art, but Devis' interpretation goes beyond this to the lay-figure's angular articulation and anatomical inconsistencies, a perfect illustration of which is *The Boldero Brothers, of Cornborough, Yorkshire* (Cat. 31). It is worth mentioning that throughout the eighteenth century it had become customary for fashionably dressed life-size dolls called 'Pandoras' to be sent regularly every month from Paris to London.[11] Members of fashionable society were therefore in part already conditioned into accepting an association of the latest mode with the lay-figure, as depicted in the paintings of Devis.

Devis' lay-figure measured about thirty inches in height. This can be determined from miniature costumes (Cat. 56 and Fig. VII, VIII) which were formerly owned by the artist. Its wardrobe originally must have been much more extensive since only one of the costumes, a hussar suit, can be identified with any known paintings, whereas it will be seen that several costumes are used repeatedly in the pictures comprising this exhibition, in particular a very fine sack and petticoat trimmed with a flounce and furbelows, which is worn by Barbara Parker (Cat. 42), one of the Clarke sisters (Cat. 45), and others. The lay-figure's wardrobe was smaller than might appear, since Devis painted the same costume in different colours, as can be seen from the sack and petticoat worn by Mrs. Miles (Cat. 41).

A remarkable feature in the paintings of Devis is the consistency of the size of the figures regardless of the dimensions of the canvas. With a few notable exceptions, standing figures range from about twelve to eighteen inches in height. Perhaps the reason for this lay in the inflexibility of his painting technique which, if it had been applied to larger-scale portraiture, would have appeared to be laboured. Conversely, there would have been much less demand for works with figures on an even smaller scale. Devis perfectly understood the limitations of his method, but also astutely appreciated that it was splendidly suited to that genre of painting in which he is now recognised as being a supreme master.

One of Devis' first tasks when painting a conversation piece was to construct an environment for his sitters. Sometimes this must have taken place even before he received their commission, as with *Robert Dashwood and his Wife, Anne, of Stamford Park, Nottinghamshire* (Cat. 18) who are seated in an interior identical to one painted three years earlier. Clearly, if his studio was in London only rarely could he be expected to travel great distances to sketch on the spot. On occasions he could have been supplied with an engraving to work from, as in the case of *Richard Streatfield, with a View of Table Bay, Cape of Good Hope, 1746* (Phot. Cooper 705288), in which the well-known shape of the mountain could have been taken from several works published by that time; he may also have used drawings — Sir Roger Newdigate (Cat. 38) is thought to have drawn him a sketch of the interior of his library; but almost invariably the settings for Devis' pictures were taken from his own imagination, and were devised with a simple purpose — to show the sitter as a "patron of art and judge of nature"

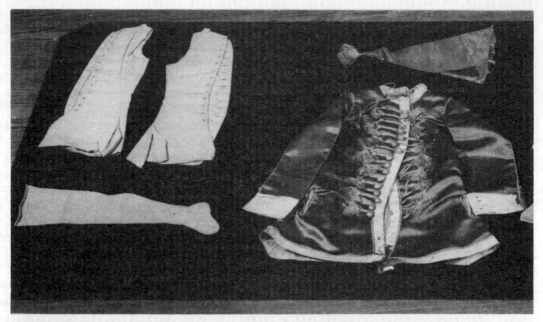

Fig VII & VIII Lay-Figure Costumes, formerly owned by Arthur Devis, c. 1755, Harris Museum and Art Gallery, (Cat. 56)

consistent with the genteel demeanour with which the artist had already invested him, and also to indicate in a simple allegorical way his personal interests.

The composition was conceived as a stage-set in which the 'actors' pose within one or more theatrical flats which, with very few exceptions, are aligned parallel to the base of the picture. In the case of interior views it represented the simplest form of perspective and could easily be drawn on a canvas using a 'T' square running along its top and side edges. The only scientific skill required was to put the measured proportions of the room into a convincing recession. A popular work which was available to Devis in his early years was *The Practice of Perspective: Or, An Easy Method of Representing Natural Objects. . .,* E. Chambers, London, 1726, which contains an engraving (Fig. IX) illustrating the method. However, as the author indicates in his introduction it was necessary for artists to understand the scientific principles involved. On occasions Devis

Fig IX   To put Chimneys in Perspective. Engraved illustration in E. Chambers, *The Practice of Perspective,* London, 1726, pl. 77 (detail). Private Collection

appears to be uncertain, particularly in the representing of the floor and desk in Sir Roger Newdigate's library (Cat. 38), and in the steeply converging lines of the architecture of Dr. Clayton's school in Salford (Cat. 9).

Devis probably gained inspiration for his interior scenes from the measured plans and elevations in architectural pattern books of the period. Just as an architect could assemble a fashionable interior from such engraved plates, with details of doors, windows, chimney-pieces, and other decorative devices, so Devis could construct the same in perspective with other furnishings added according to the wishes of his patron. Thus Roger Hesketh (Cat. 11), who is shown in an almost identical interior to that with four young children (Cat. 12), stands near a globe, has a book-case in a cartouche in the adjoining room, and a telescope on a table in a far room, all to show his scientific interests. However, the father of the four children has no such pretensions; but a painted vault in the manner of Laguerre, which Devis has substituted for Roger Hesketh's coffered ceiling, perhaps suggests a patron with Stuart sympathies. Devis, of course, could never have conceived that so many of his pictures would be brought together to be viewed at the same time, and it is significant that the owners of the two paintings lived far away from each other, in Lancashire and Dorset (See Cat. 12, note 1). Devis similarly constructed the interiors for the paintings of the *Rev. Streynsham Master and his Wife, of Croston, Lancashire* (Cat. 15) and *William Atherton and his Wife, Lucy, of Preston, Lancashire* (Cat. 14), retaining an almost identical perspective drawing of the pedestal and chimney-piece to the left, and changing the position and architectural style of the doorways on the facing walls. Other furnishings in the room may have been included at the wishes of the Rev. Master or William Atherton, but are just as likely to have been invented by the artist. Only rarely did Devis attempt a more dynamic angle of view in his interiors. Such an example is the portrait of *Assheton Curzon, later Viscount Curzon, of Penn House, Buckinghamshire with his Tutor, Dr. Mather* (Cat. 34). This striking picture is also remarkable for its unusual lighting, which can only be explained by a light source beyond the ceiling and behind the walls, and this suggests that Devis may have displayed his figures in a simple miniature stage-set consisting of the walls of a room without a ceiling. This may also explain a feature in some of his pictures, in which architectural details have the appearance of being drawn in grisaille rather than being carved or moulded.

Devis may have been influenced in his early years by the relatively obscure artist, Gawen Hamilton (c. 1697–1737), whose painting *The Earl of Strafford and his Family*[12] has close stylistic affinities with *Children in an Interior* (Cat. 12). Both paintings share a common monumental architectural style treated similarly in stage perspective, and a dramatic contrast of light and shade between the figures and their surroundings. Although such features are also to be found in other artists working at the time, notably William Hogarth and Marcellus Laroon, other aspects of the style of Devis and Hamilton, in particular the improvised placing of isolated figures across the picture plane, against a drawn rather than moulded architectural background (Cat. 18), suggests something more than the mere sharing of a common idea. Devis, it has already been said, had left Preston before 1728, and he is known to have worked either as an assistant or an apprentice to Peter Tillemans, who retired in 1733. As Gawen Hamilton was living in London from about 1730 to 1737 Devis could certainly have had the opportunity of meeting him or seeing his work. Another link may have been through Joseph Goupy who had worked with Tillemans on scenery for the Opera House, and who in 1735 owned Hamilton's well-known painting *A Club of Artists,* now at the National Portrait Gallery. Again, this picture bears some relation to Devis' *John Bacon and his Family* (Cat. 10), which was painted circa 1742–43. Where Devis differs from Hamilton is in his exacting and detailed brushwork; and yet an examination of two fragments of an unfinished conversation piece on the reverse of two of his small oval portraits (See Cat. 63 and 65) shows that his preliminary drawing was very free. In one of these (Fig. X) of the arm and dress of a seated woman, Devis has rapidly executed a preliminary drawing, and followed this with a broadly-applied dead colouring which loosely indicates the folds and substantially corrects the shape of the arm. Devis' method was then to tighten up the painting still further by using his meticulous technique to realise every detail as a miniature sculptural form in itself. There is a degree of improvisation in his method which is demonstrated by alterations which were made to his paintings while work was in progress. An examination of *Roger Hesketh and his Family* (Cat. 11) reveals the leg of a chair clearly visible through the body of a greyhound, and in the portrait of *Wrightson Mundy, of Osbaston, Leicestershire, and Markeaton, Derbyshire* (Cat.

Fig X   Arthur Devis, Fragment of an unfinished Conversation Piece, c. 1742. Harris Museum and
Art Gallery, Preston

20) Devis decided to shorten the dimensions of the pages of a letter, the original
shape of which can be seen through the landscape and tree trunk. Even more
radical changes to his portrait *Elizabeth Faulkner* (Cat. 60) in which a table
has been repainted over her costume, and her hand modified to hold a mirror.

Much of Devis' initial success in gaining commissions as a painter of
conversation pieces and small whole-length portraits must in part have been due
to the influential position of his father, Anthony, on the Town Council of Preston,
and the friendship which this gained for him with powerful sectional interests
throughout Lancashire. This was made possible because Preston, a fashionable
resort at the time, possessed unusual privileges granted by ancient royal charters
which enabled its governing body completely to control who lived and carried on
any business within the town's boundaries. It was exercised by granting the
freedom of the borough to those persons whom it was said could best serve the
interests of the town, but in eighteenth-century Preston, for reasons connected
with its political and religious history, those entrusted with the selection not only
systematically excluded applicants with known Whig sympathies, but also actively
recruited Tory sympathisers from outside the town. The reason for this was that
by selective interpretation of the wording of its charters Preston Town Council had
'established' that only freemen of the borough had a right to live in the town and

that they, and only they, were entitled to vote in parliamentary elections. Therefore, by manipulating the list of freemen, the Town Council was able to ensure the certain election of its own sponsored members of Parliament who were supporters of the Jacobite Movement.

The formal endorsing of a freeman's privileges took place at the Guild Merchant, an ancient ceremony which had been held in the town every twenty years for centuries. At that time it was the custom for every freeman to attend in person to witness his name being recorded on the Guild Roll. Only in exceptional circumstances would the town allow renewal of freedom by proxy. In September 1742 Preston was host to all the landed gentry of Lancashire and its adjoining counties, and also to rich merchants who had a financial interest in trading in the town. Arthur Devis himself was present to see his name recorded on the Guild Roll as — *"Devis, Arthur of London, Painter..."* There can be no doubt that his father would have lost no opportunity in promoting him as a fashionable London painter of conversation pieces, who would be pleased to take commissions while he was in the north. The years immediately prior to the Guild Merchant were marked by a period of activity by the Town Council in admitting those who wished to have their privileges confirmed in 1742, and among the names recorded are several persons who commissioned works from Devis at the time. These include *Roger Hesketh,* 1737 (Cat. 11), *Robert Gwillym the Younger of Langston in the County of Hereford,* 1739 (Cat. 13), *Thomas Lister of Gisburne Park,* 1740 (D'Oench, list 104), the *Rev. Streynsham Master, of Croston Church,* 1740 (Cat. 15), and the *Rev. William Farington, Vicar of Leigh,* 1741 (Cat. 7). In addition, other members of the Town Council and their friends and relations added to Devis' commissions. These included William Atherton (Cat. 14), Ralph Assheton (Cat. 8), John Clayton (Cat. 9) who was a friend of Ralph Assheton, Wrightson Mundy (Cat. 20) who was related to the Molyneux family of Preston, and Thomas Starkie (Cat. 21). However, most of those who commissioned Arthur Devis through his Preston associations tended to be Jacobite supporters, and so indeed were other friends to whom they had recommended Devis, and who included Robert Dashwood (Cat. 18), John Lockwood (Cat. 36), and probably Sir Roger Newdigate (Cat. 38). By accident or design, therefore, Devis found himself reliant upon Jacobite sympathisers for his livelihood, and this would appear to be confirmed by the double portrait miniature (Cat. 66) said to represent his own portrait and that of Prince Charles Edward. This must to some extent have alienated Devis not only from his colleagues working in London, but also from potential patrons. Certainly for so skilful an artist it is strange that there are so few contemporary references to him. Neither Horace Walpole nor Joseph Farington refer to him in their voluminous writings, and it is extraordinary that his name should have been omitted from a list of fifty-six painters of portraits and conversation pieces working in England, published in *The Universal Magazine* for November, 1748. There is also the clear evidence afforded by the original geographical location of his known pictures, which shows a great proportion to have been painted for patrons in Lancashire, Cheshire and Derbyshire, counties which had powerful families actively promoting the Stuart cause, comparatively few in the immediate vicinity of London, and the rest evenly distributed throughout England. This distribution also indicated that the prejudices of Lord John Cavendish (See Cat. 40) concerning the merits of Devis' paintings were apparently held by most members of fashionable London society during the artist's career.

There is a remarkable consistency in Devis' technical methods throughout his career, and the same careful attention to minute detail and textural effects so evident in *John Bacon and his Family,* 1742-43 (Cat. 10) can also be seen in one of his last great conversation piece paintings, *Edward Rookes-Leeds and his Family, of Royds Hall, Low Moor, Yorkshire,* 1763–68 (Cat. 51). Nevertheless, there are clear stylistic developments in his art which demonstrate not only his familiarity with the works of other artists of his day, but also at times an originality of ideas which others were later to exploit. His earliest conversation pieces are characterised by figures in monumental settings with dramatic contrasts of light and shadow. There is also a sense of movement, not present in his later works, which derives from a strongly pronounced shadow falling diagonally across the composition. Two fine examples of this are *Roger Hesketh and his Family* (Cat. 11) and *Children in an Interior* (Cat. 12), which can be compared with paintings executed in the 1730s by an older generation of artists, in particular William Hogarth, Marcellus Laroon and Gawen Hamilton. Another painting, somewhat earlier, is *Breaking-up Day at Dr. Clayton's School in Salford* (Cat. 9), in which Devis emphasises the theatrical nature of the scene by placing the learned doctor on a diagonally-stepped plinth, and by cutting away part of the interior to allow the narrative to take place inside and outside the school. All three paintings have an archaism about them which would probably have appeared outmoded in London in the early 1740s, and it is significant that Devis rapidly abandoned the style for a more intimate portrayal of figures in their surroundings. The *Rev. Streynsham Master and his Wife, of Croston, Lancashire* (Cat. 15), which again dates from the early 1740s, has a lightness and grace more in keeping with the spirit of the rococo. Devis has reduced the architectural scale of the interior, has exchanged the dramatic tonal contrasts so apparent in earlier paintings for a more evenly distributed lighting, and has developed a more static composition. Accompanying this is a fresher palette of shimmering blues, red browns, and silvery greys. Another feature is the introduction of furnishings which emphasise the fashionable nature of the interior – a French ormolu clock on a rococo side table, with an Italianate landscape over the mantelpiece. The same may be said of the *The Duet* (Cat. 17), painted in 1749, in which Devis identifies the unknown couple with the latest architectural mode in a Palladian window which dominates the composition. The picture is also a magnificent example of Devis' craftsmanship, with splendidly realised textures of satin and polished mahogany, offset by simple flat tones of the walls and floor. Devis' subtle use of colour, so evident in this painting, can also be appreciated in three small whole-length portraits from the same period – *Miss Sarah Tyssen of Hackney, Middlesex* (Cat. 22), *Lady in a Blue Dress* (Cat. 23), and *Lucy Watson* (Cat. 24). This period also marks a new phase in Devis' stylistic development with the doll-like characteristics of the lay-figure being used as an art form in itself. The astonishing leaning posture assumed by Mr. Van Harthals (Cat. 27), and the elongated and angular forms of the Boldero Brothers (Cat. 31), are extreme examples of a mannerist aspect in his art which recurred at regular intervals throughout his career.

In the early 1750s Devis' paintings were transformed by a short-lived romantic phase in which the principal action is concentrated by a strong chiaroscuro and a severe restrain in the use of colour. An outstanding example of this is the portrait *Assheton Curzon with his tutor, Dr. Roger Mather* (Cat. 34), in which the figures are presented as on a stage, illuminated by a light source above and beyond the interior in which they are standing. Dr. Mather is caught in a fleeting moment indicating the meaning of a passage in a book which he is holding, while his pupil looks intently towards him. The psychological relationship between tutor and pupil is altogether different from that in any other painting by Devis, and contrasts in its approach with a similar theme in *Breaking-up Day at Dr. Clayton's School in Salford* (Cat. 9). While in the latter the spectator becomes a participant in the end-of-term ceremony, in the former he eavesdrops on the two men who are unaware of his presence. Other paintings of the period demonstrate an attempt by the artist to capture something of the personality of the sitter, rather than his outward appearance based on material possessions and a polite demeanour. Thus, Sir Roger Newdigate (Cat. 38) is shown musing detachedly in his part-completed library, John Lockwood (Cat. 35) is given a languid and introspective appearance, while his wife, Matilda (Cat. 36), adopts a pose of pensive and poetic melancholy. Ellen D'Oench has drawn attention to the probable influence on Devis of Benjamin Wilson, a successful portrait painter who lived near him in Great Queen Street, and who exploited effects of chiaroscuro not unlike those found in this short-lived phase of Devis. Such an association between the two artists is even more convincing when it is considered that Wilson settled in London in 1750, shortly before Devis' paintings were executed. Ten years later the same method was adopted by Joseph Wright of Derby in his well-known paintings *A Philosopher giving a Lecture on the Orrery* (c. 1763–65) and *An Experiment on a Bird in the Air Pump* (1768).

The later 1750s account for some of Devis' greatest works, in particular *Edward Parker and his Wife, Barbara (née Fleming), on the Terrace at Browsholme Hall, near Clitheroe* (Cat. 42), which represents a new breadth of scale with classical overtones. A similar spatial awareness can also be seen in *Col. John Sabine, and his Family, in the Park at Tewin House, Hertfordshire* (Cat. 44), in which the artist has monumentalised his sitters by placing them well above the line of the horizon on a vast undulating lawn. A small whole-length portrait from this period is *Richard Lowe, Esq., of Denby and Locko Park, Derbyshire* (Cat. 48). Here Devis has invested Richard Lowe with a grace and dignity which suggests that he was experimenting with new concepts in the closing years of his career. Such digressions, however, had no permanence, and two of his greatest works from his last years, *Alicia and Jane Clarke, of Walford Court, Ross-on-Wye, Herefordshire* (Cat. 45) and *Edward Rookes-Leeds and his Family, of Royds Hall, Low Moor, Yorkshire* (Cat. 51), exhibit all those characteristics of decorative richness and superlative craftsmanship, which are common features in his earlier paintings.

The last twenty years of Devis' career, prior to his retirement in 1783, sadly represent him as an artist unwilling or unable to accommodate himself to new aesthetic theories which had evolved as a reaction against rococo art. To the later generation of artists, whose aims were truth to nature, boldness of form, and nobility of concept, Devis' figure compositions with their delicately affected poses and calculated politeness, represented an abstracted remoteness from real life which belonged to a vanished age. Devis himself must in part have recognised this, and evidence suggests that he diversified his studio practice to include restoration. As early as 1762 he had been employed by Sir Roger Newdigate to restore and enlarge ancestral portraits at Arbury Hall, and in 1777 he was commissioned to repair and restore the Painted Hall at Greenwich.

It is also during this period that we are offered a rare glimpse of Devis' relations with his fellow artists. As early as 1745–46 a group of artists which included William Hogarth, Francis Hayman, Joseph Highmore, and Thomas

Hudson, among others, had joined together in donating examples of their work to the Foundling Hospital. [13] Having been elected governors of the institution, they were given permission to hold annual business meetings there, and in effect formed the first artists' society in London. Devis was either not invited or chose not to join the circle, and years later in 1760, when it held its first exhibition in the Great Room of the Society for the Encouragement of Arts, Manufactures, and Commerce, he did not appear in the catalogue. However, it is significant that he assumed a major rôle the following year when, because of internal dissension, the most talented artists left to form what became known as the Society of Artists. Two exhibitions were held in 1761, one by the seceders, and the other by the group of which Devis was a member, again at the same premises as in the previous year. It is interesting that Devis also joined the Society for the Encouragement of Arts, Manufactures, and Commerce on May 13, 1761,[14] shortly after the exhibition opened in their Great Room in April. The proceeds of the exhibition amounted to £150, to be divided equally in charitable donations to Middlesex Hospital, the British Lying-in Hospital, and the Asylum for Female Orphans. Devis was chosen to hand £50 to the latter asylum, and was elected to its board of governors in perpetuity. In 1763 the society adopted the name 'The Free Society of Artists,' and regularly held exhibitions until 1783. Notwithstanding the poor standard of works on display compared with those painted by members of the rival 'Society of Artists,' Devis remained loyal, exhibiting twenty-six paintings between the years 1761 and 1780, and being elected President of the society in 1768.

On April 7, 1783, *The Morning Herald* and *Daily Advertiser* carried notices that J. Sanders, Jnr. was "taking over the House and business of Mr. Devis, who is retired into the country." Devis retired to Brighton, where he died in obscurity on July 25, 1787. His obituary notice in the *Gentleman's Magazine* was confined to one line — *"At Brighthelmstone, Arthur Davis, esq."* In 1808 Edward Edwards included a brief biography of Devis in his *Anecdotes of painters,* where he described him in carefully chosen words as *"having supported the character of a respectable artist."*[15] Throughout the nineteenth century his works were all but ignored, and it is only now, in the perspective of time, that he can be seen as one of the foremost exponents of the art of the conversation piece in England.

Perhaps to supplement his income Devis is known to have taken on students at his Great Queen Street Studio. Only four can be identified, as follows:—

i. George Senhouse, who was apprenticed to Devis from July 7, 1752, to March 1755, when. because of his idleness, his master was obliged to dispense with him. George Senhouse, an unstable character, was declared insane in 1759, and was committed to Billington Mental Asylum, Lancashire.[16] No works by him are known to exist.

ii. Robert Marris (1750–1827), who exhibited in 1770 at the Free Society from Devis' address. Interestingly, Robert Marris was later to marry Frances, second surviving daughter of Devis. One of their daughters, Ellin Devis Marris, later married Dr. Martin Tupper, father of Martin Farquhar Tupper (See Cat. 66, note 1).

iii. Master Maynard, an unknown artist, who exhibited at the Free Society in 1770 two paintings, *A deception* and *A painting in imitation of a metzotinto,* which are identical titles to those entered by Marris in the same year. It is not surprising that Horace Walpole should have made a note in his catalogue for that year "this was a very bad Exhibition, with scarce a tolerable picture..."[17]

iv. His last known student was Chandois, an unknown artist who was at Devis' address as late as 1780, when he entered a painting in the Free Society exhibition.

The distribution of dates from the early 1750s to 1780 suggests that Devis may have had other students who have gone unrecorded.

Devis also had two sons, Thomas Anthony (1757–1810) and Arthur William (1762–1822) (Cat. 62), both of whom he trained as artists, and who exhibited at the Free Society in the 1770s.

Fig XI   Model Tomb, c. 1788, Harris Museum and Art Gallery, Preston, (Cat. 67)

He is also thought to have collaborated with the animal painter, James Seymour (c. 1702–52). It has been suggested by Ellen D'Oench and Basil Taylor that in Devis' painting of *Leak Okeover, the Rev. John Allen, and Capt. Chester, in the Grounds of Okeover Hall, Staffordshire,* horses and dogs have been added by Seymour.[18] There is also an almost identical drawing of a tree on the left of Devis' portrait of *Robert Gwillym of Atherton, and William Farington, of Shawe Hall, Lancashire,* 1743, at Yale University Art Gallery, to one similarly placed in a painting *The Coursing Party* by Seymour, reproduced in the Sotheby sale catalogue of the collection of Mr. and Mrs. Jack R. Dick, April 28, 1976 (185).

Perhaps even more interesting is the possible rôle of his half-brother Anthony Devis[19] (1729–1816) (Cat. 61 and 64) who, as early as 1742, is recorded in the Preston Guild Merchant roll of freemen as *Anthony, his* (Arthur's) *half brother, of London, Painter.* It is not known where he was living in London until twenty years later, in 1762, when he shared an address with his brother, John (Cat. 65), at 16 Gloucester Street, Bloomsbury. It is astonishing that there are apparently no paintings which can be ascribed to him dating from the period 1742 to the early 1760s, by which time he clearly was a proficient artist, for in 1763 he was awarded the Free Society's third premium of ten guineas for landscape painting. Anthony Devis' rare landscape paintings in oil show affinities with the landscape backgrounds in some of Arthur's paintings, and this raises the question of whether the two artists may have collaborated in joint productions.

An artist whose works are often confused with those of Arthur Devis is the virtually unknown Edward Haytley (fl. c. 1740–1765). Haytley, like Devis, had strong links with Lancashire; he painted six small whole-length portraits of members of the Earl of Derby's family at Knowsley Hall, near Liverpool; he shared with Devis the patronage of William Farington of Shawe Hall, Leyland, near Preston; and also worked for Sir Roger Bradshaigh of Haigh Hall. In addition, both Devis and Haytley received commissions from Sir William Milner of Nun Appleton Hall, Yorkshire; Devis painting his wife, Lady Milner (née Mordaunt), in 1760, and Haytley matching this with a pendant of Sir William in 1764.

There are, however, stylistic differences in the method of the two artists. Haytley's works are comparatively broadly handled, with less attention given to minute details and textures. This can be seen to advantage in the painting of *Sir Roger and Lady Bradshaigh, of Haigh Hall, Lancashire* (Cat. 54), in which the costume of Lady Bradshaigh is rapidly and spontaneously executed, the architectural details of Haigh Hall lightly touched in, and the foliage of the tree painted to give a general impression rather than, as in Devis' case, a reconstruction of every leaf and branch. Haytley's method is also matched by the animation in his painting – a parrot perches on the back of a chair, the dog turns to look at its master, and a lady and gentleman in a rowing boat sail into the picture. It is also true of almost all his known works, that the figures in them are more convincingly real in their proportions and attitudes, and this demonstrates less reliance on the use of the lay-figure. The last years have seen the discovery of several important works by Haytley, in particular the magnificent conversation piece, *The Montagu Family.*[20] Perhaps other paintings still to be found may give a clue to his elusive association with Devis.

Stephen V. Sartin

1. Unfortunately, some records for the area before 1710 have been lost, and the date of Anthony's birth and marriage are not known. The MS Court Leet records for October 9, 1709 show that Anthony was not in Preston to attend jury service in the preceding months, and it may well be that he was working away from the town in the area of Whitewell, where he met and married Ellin Rauthmell. The Devis family could already have known the Rauthmells; Whitewell is not far away from the Cockerham, Forton, Garstang area from where the Devis family originated.

2. This may be deduced from his appearing as a juror in Preston Court Leet on October 1, 1708. Only Free-Inn-Burgesses (freemen of the borough) and persons who had served an apprenticeship in the town would have been called. Anthony Devis was not a freeman at the time. Although there is no record of him being an apprentice, on October 5, 1704, James Verscragen, one of the leading cabinet makers in the town, was summoned along with others for failing to give town officials the names of his apprentices.

3. In that year Anthony Devis was appointed 'houselooker' for Church Street. Houselookers were appointed to enforce the strict rules of the Town Council that no strangers entered the town to live there. They always lived in the area designated to them. The Devis family must have been living at the same address in 1708 when Robert, a relative of Anthony, and almost certainly his father, was found to be living illegally in Church Street, and was ordered out of Preston. A Robert Devis, son of John Devis of Park Lane, Cockerham, was born on February 7, 1658, and married Ann Gardner at Cockerham in 1685.

4. MS Court Leet Records, Feb. 20, 1720 – "We present Anthony Devis for laying wood in Churchgate to ye annoyance of the street and do amerce him 6s.8d."

5. He was present to be enrolled as a Free-Inn-Burgess (the right of all sons of freemen of the borough) at the Preston Guild Merchant of September 1722, but was not in the town in 1728 when he would automatically have become liable for jury service.

6. See MS catalogue of paintings at Knowsley Hall, 1729 (Knowsley Hall) in which are mentioned "Three Views from the Sumer House." These are by Tillemans. For further information see Robert Raines, 'Peter Tillemans, Life and Work, with a list of representative paintings, Walpole Society, 1978'-80, pp.21–59, with reprs. pl.9a–19d.'

7. Edward Edwards, Anecdotes of Painters who have resided or been born in England, London, 1808, p.122.

8. Robert Raines, note 6, for a transcription of the catalogue.

9. Samuel Richardson, Pamela: or, Virtue Rewarded, 4 vol. 3rd edit., London, 1742.

10. John Ingamells and Robert Raines, 'A Catalogue of the Paintings, Drawings and Etchings of Philip Mercier,' Walpole Society, vol. 46, 1978, pp.1–70, repr. pl.56.

11. Max von Boehm, Modes and Manners, vol. 4, The Eighteenth Century, London, 1935, pp.150–52.

12. Sacheverell Sitwell, Conversation Pieces. A Survey of English Domestic Portraits and their Painters, London, 1936, repr. opp. p.72.

13. For further information on this and on the subsequent exhibitions of the 'Society of Artists' and the 'Free Society of Artists,' see Algernon Graves, The Society of Artists of Great Britain, 1760–1791, The Free Society of Artists, 1761–1783, Dictionary of Contributors, London, 1907, pp.295–341.

14. I am indebted to Dr. D. G. C. Allan, of the Royal Society of Arts for kindly supplying me with this information.

15. Note 7.

16. For further information see D'Oench, pp.34–37, and Edward Hughes, North Country Life In the Eighteenth Century, 2 vol. London, 1952, and 1965, vol. 2, pp.89–101.

17. 'Notes by Horace Walpole, fourth Earl of Orford, on the Exhibitions of the Society of Artists and the Free Society of Artists,' 1760–91, Ed. Hugh Gatty, Walpole Society, vol. 27, 1938–39, p.84.

18. For further information on Seymour's possible rôle in this painting see D'Oench, Cat. 16.

19. Anthony, Arthur's father had married Ann Blackburn, daughter of John Blackburn of Friarhead, Gargrave, and Marrick Abbey, near Richmond, following the death of his first wife, Ellin Rauthmell, in July 1727. Ann Blackburn was a cousin of Thomas Lister of Gisburne Park near Clitheroe, and was also related to the Parker family of Browsholme Hall. See MS pedigree of the descendands of Col. Francis Malham. Pavière collection of papers relating to Devis, Witt Library.

20. See the catalogue of the exhibition English Eighteenth Century Paintings, Leger Galleries, London, June-July, 1978, for further information on this painting and a monograph on Haytley with a preliminary catalogue of his then known works.

Catalogue of exhibits

Notes on Catalogue Entries

Apart from several small portraits and miniatures the general arrangement of paintings by Devis is in chronological sequence. Measurements are given in inches, with height preceding width. Where works are described as signed, this refers to the artist's holograph.

The two principal reference works – Sydney H. Pavière, *The Devis Family of Painters,* F. Lewis, Publishers, Ltd., Leigh-on-Sea, 1950; and Ellen G. D'oench, catalogue of the exhibition *The Conversation Piece: Arthur Devis and His Contemporaries,* Yale Center for British Art, New Haven, 1980, have been abbreviated to 'Pavière' followed by his catalogue number, and 'D'Oench' followed by either the exhibition catalogue number of the list number of 281 works by Devis which she added for reference.

All catalogue entries are included as black and white plates or colour reproductions. Several supporting illustrations are also included in the text of the other sections.

Limited availability of several paintings, and restrictions on space at the National Portrait Gallery has meant that some catalogue entries will not be exhibited at both venues. The following abbreviations have therefore been appended to each entry:–

P for Preston only; *NPG* for National Portrait Gallery only.

1. Self-Portrait   c. 1737

Canvas, 27 × 22½ in.
Harris Museum and Art Gallery, Preston

Arthur Devis is known to have painted four self-portraits,[1] of which this is the earliest, dating from c. 1737. Here he is shown at the beginning of his career as a portrait painter, following the disbandment of Peter Tilleman's studio in 1733.

1. The other three are represented in the exhibition as Cat. 2, 33, and 58. There are also four portraits of Arthur Devis executed by other artists, who include Anthony Devis, Cat. 61, Richard Corbould, shown here as part of the furnishings of the model tomb, Cat. 67, a double-portrait miniature of Prince Charles Edward and Devis, Cat. 66, and a miniature of him at the age of 53 by an unidentified artist not in the exhibition.

PROVENANCE: Devis family; purchased from a descendant c. 1900; Christie's, December 2, 1949, purchased by Harris Museum and Art Gallery.

REFERENCES: Pavière (Addenda p.64); D'Oench, list 47, and p.17, repr. Fig. 6.

2. Self-Portrait   1742

Canvas, 30 × 25 in.
Harris Museum and Art Gallery, Preston

When the painting was re-lined in 1936 a small piece of card was found between the canvas and the stretcher, inscribed *I Give this Picture/to my Grandson/Thomas Devis.*[1] On the canvas was an inscription *The Gift of Arthur Devis/to/his Father, Anthony Devis/1742.*[2]

1. According to Pavière this is probably the portrait mentioned by Martin F. Tupper in his book *My Life as an Author*, London, 1886, p.207, as being then at Albury, the home of Anthony, half-brother to Arthur.

2. Photograph in archives of Harris Museum and Art Gallery.

PROVENANCE: Probably by descent to Mrs. C. Tupper; anonymous sale, Christie's, Dec. 21, 1928 (14), and anonymous sale, Christie's, April 3, 1936 (91), bought in on both occasions as Anthony Devis, Arthur's father; with Brook Street Galleries, London, 1936, purchased by Harris Museum and Art Gallery, 1936.

EXHIBITED: Preston, *Lancashire Art*, 1937 (17), repr. in cat.

REFERENCES: Pavière (33); D'Oench, list 49; *The Lancashire Daily Post*, July 4, 1936; S. H. Pavière, 'Biographical Notes on the Devis Family of Painters,' *Walpole Society*, vol.25, 1936–37, repr. pl.43b *Illustrated London News* 190 (March 20, 1937), p.530; *The Sphere* 148 (March 20, 1937), p.451; *Country Life* 81 (March 13, 1937), repr. pl.60.

3. Hoghton Tower from Duxon Hill, Lancashire   1735

Canvas, 40 × 50 in.
Private Collection

This painting, commissioned by Sir Henry Hoghton in 1735,[1] clearly shows the influence exerted on Devis by his master, Peter Tillemans (Cat. 4), particularly in the choice of a panoramic view in the composition, and a Flemish approach to detail which extends even to including a coach and horses on the approach to Hoghton Tower, when in reality it would hardly be visible to the artist from Duxon Hill. A further similarity between the two artists lies in the use of thin transparent colour with comparatively little body in it.[2]

Devis' careful observation of topographical features in the landscape makes this painting a valuable local historical record. The large 16th century stone-built manor house is shown dominating the summit of Hoghton Hill. The formal shape of the trees and shrubs on the approach to the Tower reflects the introduction of the Dutch fashion of landscape gardening after the Restoration. Outside the Tower quadrangle is the large barn built in 1692 which still exists. The rest of the Tower buildings appear in the painting much as they do at present. The footpath in the immediate foreground passes through Wards o' th' Hill farmyard to join the old Preston to Blackburn road.

Sir Henry Hoghton (c. 1679–1768) was a Whig politician who represented Preston — an unusual constituency with two sitting members of Parliament — in the years 1710–13, 1715–22, and 1727–41. His strongly non-conformist religious principles made him one of the most active opponents of the Jacobites in Lancashire, and as deputy lieutenant of the county he played a crucial rôle in the armed forces during the rebellion of 1715. Again in 1745 he was in the forefront of opposition to the Young Pretender. In a letter written to Pelham[3] on the military situation in the county he indicated that "We have some friends but few in comparison to those against us ... I can't end this without asking pardon for differing in opinion that the dispositions of the people and the strength of the enemy is far different from what it was in the year 1715. As to our own county, our enemies are as strong as then, and I know of no converts to be depended on." He was correct in his estimation. Prince Charles Edward led the rebel army into Preston on November 27, 1745 without opposition. His father was proclaimed King of Great Britain before crowds in the Market Place, and the rebel chiefs attended a banquet held in their honour at the White Bull Inn.[4]

1. LRO (DD Ho 10), MS account book showing the *"disbursements of William Anderson, gent., for the use of Sir Henry Hoghton, bart.,"* – Feb. 11th 1734/5, *"To Mr. Art. Devis for Drawing a view of Hoghton tower p accnt £6.6s."*

2. Many signatures on Devis' paintings have become indecipherable or even erased altogether because of his use of thin colour.

3. Romney Sedgwick, *The History of Parliament: The House of Commons, 1715–54* H.M.S.O. London 1970), vol.2, pp.143–144.

4. Charles Hardwick, *History of the Borough of Preston and its Environs* (Preston 1857), p.242.

PROVENANCE: By descent to the present owner.

REFERENCES: Pavière (68); D'Oench, list 270.

4. Uppark, West Sussex,   c. 1725
Peter Tillemans   (c. 1684–1734)   P

Canvas, 16¼ × 35½ in.
Private Collection

This landscape by Peter Tillemans is included in the exhibition to show how Devis was able so successfully to imitate the style of his master at the earliest stage of his career.[1]

Tillemans, an Antwerp artist, came to England in the first decade of the 18th century, where he became popular for his plagiarisms of the works of Borgonone, Teniers, and others. He is, however, remembered more for his topographical landscapes in which his Flemish eye for detail suited English patrons, who wished to record their country seats, hunting scenes and horse racing. He travelled widely throughout England, and it is probable that Devis could have first met him on his visit to Knowsley Hall in the 1720s.[2]

The only known works executed by Devis as an assistant to Tillemans are landscapes after Marco Ricci, Giovanni Paolo Pannini, and Jan van Bloemen.[3] *Hoghton Tower from Duxon Hill* (Cat. 3) is unique in Devis' oeuvre in so closely imitating the style of Tillemans himself. This inevitably raises the question of whether Devis could have been the author of some paintings more doubtfully attributed to his master.

1. See Robert Raines, Peter Tillemans, Life and Work, with a list of representative Paintings, *Walpole Society*, 1980, list 41, repr. pl.15a.

2. Hamlet Winstanley, who had several patrons living in Preston and almost certainly knew Anthony Devis, Arthur's father, was working at Knowsley Hall and could have acted as an intermediary between the Devis family and Tillemans.

3. See the sale catalogue of paintings owned by Peter Tillemans, April 19, 20, 1733, British Library SC213/4, repr. in Walpole Society, 1980, pp. 34–38.

PROVENANCE: By descent to the present owner.

REFERENCES: Walpole Society, see note 1.

5. John Orlebar, of Hinwick House, Bedfordshire   c. 1740

Canvas, 20 × 14 in.
Private Collection

John Orlebar was born in 1697, the son of John Orlebar of Red Lion Square, London, and Elizabeth, daughter of John Whitfield of Maidenhead, Berkshire. He was educated at Eton and King's College, Cambridge, and became like his father a bencher of the Middle Temple. In 1738 he was offered the post of Commissioner of Excise which he held until his death in 1765. In 1727 he was returned as a Whig member of Parliament for Bedford and voted consistently with the Administration in all recorded divisions until he vacated the seat in 1734.[1]

Here he is shown, leaning elegantly against a small bureau, magnificently attired in a grey coat, gold-embroidered waistcoat, and grey breeches. In his right hand he holds an immaculately-pressed pair of gloves, clearly regarded by him as an ornament to his person rather than of any utilitarian value.

This comparatively early work is a straightforward portrait study in which Devis has yet to adopt the aesthetic niceties so apparent later in his career. The bureau to the right, unique in his paintings, may have belonged to Sir John Orlebar who required it to be included in his portrait.

1. Romney Sedgwick, *The History of Parliament, The House of Commons, 1715–54*, (H.M.S.O. London 1970), vol.2, p.313.

PROVENANCE: A label on the reverse reads *"This portrait of my Grandfather John Orlebar, I give to my great nephew Richard Orlebar. W. A. Orlebar, 1854;"* Viscountess Cowdray; the Hon. Mrs. Murray, 1948; by descent to the present owner.

EXHIBITED: London, *English Conversation Pieces*, 1930 (102); Preston. *Lancashire Art*, 1937 (21).

REFERENCES: Pavière (112); G. C. Williamson, *English Conversation Pictures*, B. T. Batsford Ltd. (London 1931), pl.xxvii.

6. John Orlebar, of Hinwick House, Bedfordshire   c. 1740   P

Canvas, 20 × 14 in.
Harris Museum and Art Gallery, Preston

This portrait, a pendant to the previous catalogue entry, shows Sir John Orlebar seated at a tripod table, wearing a brown coat, gold-embroidered red waistcoat, and black breeches. He holds in his hand a letter which it is tempting to suggest may be associated with his becoming Commissioner of Excise in 1738. If this is the case it would certainly agree with the date c. 1740 when he would have received the two portraits from Devis.

A feature common to both portraits is the artist's unsure drawing of the floor tiles in which the perspective, at this early stage in his career, is more intuitive than calculated.

PROVENANCE: This portrait and the previous catalogue entry, at one time together in the same collection, may have become separated when W. A. Orlebar presented the portrait of his grandfather, standing, to his great nephew Richard Orlebar in 1854; Brook Street Galleries, London, 1935; purchased by the Harris Museum and Art Gallery.

EXHIBITED: Preston, *Lancashire Art*,   1935 (6); Preston. *Lancashire Art*, 1937 (22).

REFERENCES: Pavière (111).

7. The Rev. William Farington, of Leigh, Lancashire   c. 1741–42   P

Inscribed in a later hand along the lower edge – "*Wm. Farington, Vicar of Leigh 1733, Rector of Warrington 1767 when he died Aged 63.*"
Canvas 20 × 14 in.
Harris Museum and Art Gallery, Preston

The link between Arthur Devis and the Farington family, already established by his father as a member of Preston Town Council earlier in the century, did much to determine the nature of the patronage he was to receive during his artistic career; for in painting the portraits of the Faringtons, and their relations in the Atherton, Lister, and Parker families, he was identifying himself with some of the most prominent names associated with the Jacobite cause in Lancashire.

The Rev. William Farington was born in 1704 and educated at Brasenose College, Oxford. Through the interest of the Atherton family he was installed as Vicar of Leigh in 1733, a living which he held until 1767, the year of his death. In 1744 he married an heiress, Esther Gilbody of Manchester, who had money "but no arms to decorate the Farington pedigree." He died shortly after being presented to the Rectory of Warrington in 1767, leaving £1200. If he himself had little interest in the visual arts he certainly encouraged his children to take up painting as a profession. He was the father of the landscape painter, Joseph Farington, R.A., and also of George Farington, a history painter who had studied under Benjamin West.

Here he is shown as Vicar of Leigh, penning a letter or sermon at a tripod table. The monumental interior with pedimented chimney-piece and hanging drapery is an early example of a compositional format which with modifications Devis retained in his portraits throughout his career.

PROVENANCE: By descent to Henry Nowell Farington, of Worden Hall, Leyland, near Preston; bt. Harris Museum and Art Gallery, 1948.

EXHIBITED: Preston, *Lancashire Art*, 1935 (115); Preston, *Lancashire Art*, 1937 (25).

REFERENCES: Pavière (38); D'Oench, list 58; repr. *The Times*, March 27, 1935.

8. Ralph Assheton, of Cuerdale Hall, near Preston, Lancashire   1742   P

An inscription on the reverse gives the names of Ralph Assheton and Arthur Devis with the date
Canvas, 18 × 12½ in.
Private Collection

Ralph Assheton (1719–1759), Lord of the Manors of Cuerdale and Downham, was descended from the ancient family of that name which derived from Ashton-under-Lyne. He married Rebecca, elder daughter of William Hulls of Freelands, Co. Kent, and Popes in the County of Hertford, at Westminster Abbey on August 8, 1752. He was the son of Edmund Assheton, a wealthy Preston mercer, who held the prestigious office of Guild Mayor in 1722, and for several years served on the Town Council with Anthony Devis, Arthur's father. Through his mother, Mary, he was the grandson of Thomas Lister of Gisburne, a Tory member of Parliament for Clitheroe (1713–45), and a consistent opponent of the Government.[1]

Educated at Westminster and Balliol College, Oxford, here he is portrayed as the cultivated owner of Cuerdale Hall, Preston. On a table to his right is a flute placed on some sheets of music. With head erect he adopts an easy, cross-legged stance, the toes of his shoes almost touching. His left arm falls gently by his side, his hand disdaining the informality of being thrust into his coat pocket.

Beyond, over the chimney-piece, is an Italianate landscape which recalls Devis' early years as an assistant to Peter Tillemans, when he was required to copy works by Marco Ricci. The interior, which is common to other works by Devis, bears no resemblance to Cuerdale Hall, which still exists as a farmhouse, and it is more than likely that the artist made a portrait study in Preston, when he was there to attend the Guild Merchant of 1742, and then executed the picture at his studio in Great Queen Street, London.

A feature common to many portraits by Devis is the column on a pedestal to the right, which, with the hanging drapery to the left, lends a severe symmetry to the composition.

1. Romney Sedgwick, *The History of Parliament, The House of Commons, 1715–54*, (H.M.S.O. London, 1970), vol.2, p.219.

PROVENANCE: By descent to the present owner.

REFERENCES: Pavière (4); D'Oench, list 5.

9. Breaking-up Day at Dr. Clayton's School in Salford   c. 1738–40

Inscribed '– Nunc adbibe puro/Pectore Verba Puer –' on scroll held by Dr. Clayton. A now illegible inscription was on the cartouche affixed to the wall to the left of him.
Canvas, 47½ × 68¾ in.
Tate Gallery, London

This picture was for many years at Kersall Cell, Broughton, near Manchester, the home of the Byrom family. It was almost certainly commissioned by the poet and stenographer John Byrom (1692–1763) whose son, Edward, is shown seated on the steps in the left foreground. In 1891 it was described by the Rev. F. R. Raines[1] as "a large historical picture ... of the interior of Mr. Clayton's school in Salford, and a full-length portrait of the Master, in a blue velvet gown lined with white silk, hearing the boys recite their pieces previous to the breaking up for the holidays ... The portraits are all likenesses, but unfortunately are unknown ... Edward Byrom, son of the doctor, is the little boy seated cross-legged on a stool, and the tradition is

that the piece being recited by the lad standing before Mr. Clayton is Byrom's poem of 'The Three Black Crows'[2] which was originally written for the Grammar School." Clayton holds in his hand a scroll with a quotation from Horace's Epistles which translated reads "Now drink in these words with a pure heart, boy ..."[3]

John Clayton (1709–73) was educated at Manchester Grammar School and Brasenose College, Oxford, where he joined John Wesley and others in founding the society of Oxford Methodists. He returned to Lancashire in 1732 as curate of Trinity Church, Salford, where he lost his enthusiasm for Methodism and adopted high-church practices. He also became a propagandist for the Jacobite cause.[4] Not surprisingly, when he founded a private school in the mid 1730s it gained the support of similarly-minded county gentry who wished their sons to be educated according to his strict academic, religious, and political principles.

Also quoted as having been included in the painting is Richard Assheton, one of Clayton's favourite pupils[5] and brother of Ralph Assheton of Cuerdale Hall, near Preston (Cat. 8). On the evidence that Clayton accepted students from childhood at least to 16 years of age, the inclusion of Edward Byrom (b. 1724) and Richard Assheton (b. 1727) suggests that among the other students are Sir Darcy Lever, Roger Sedgwick (son of a Salford overseer to the poor), and possibly Richard,[6] son of Christopher Hartley of Marton-in-Craven, all of whom are known to have studied with Clayton. The man seated to the right wearing a pink gown may be John Byrom.

This important painting, ambitious in scale and monumental in concept, presents Clayton's school as a stage-set in which both interior and exterior can be viewed at the same time. Devis' choice of architecture,[7] made more heroic by its projection in perspective, is essentially baroque. So too is the way in which Clayton, standing on a plinth surrounded by scientific instruments,[8] is the subject of such tribute from his students and patron.

Here, seen in microcosm, is the society from which Arthur Devis gained his patrons for much of his career.

1. Rev. F. R. Raines, M.A., Hon. Canon of Manchester Cathedral, The Fellows of the Collegiate Church of Manchester, *The Chetham Society*, 1891, pt.II, p.257. This is a longer version of a description of the painting given in 1855 by Richard Parkinson (see References) quoting from a now lost MS. Since the phrases are almost identical it is probable that Raines himself was using the same source which at one time may have included a key to all the sitters in the painting.

2. 'The Three Black Crows,' quoted in full in The Poems of John Byrom, *The Chetham Society*, 1894, vol.I, pp.151–155, was originally written to be spoken by students at the beginning of the vacation of Manchester Grammar School. It was suitably modified and used in Clayton's school on the same occasion. It consists of a warning to students to be wary of unfounded rumours which change in their content the more often they are told.

3. Translation kindly supplied by Fabia Egerton.

4. When Prince Charles Edward passed through Salford with his rebel army it is said that Clayton fell upon his knees before him and "invoked a divine blessing upon the young Prince."

5. Rev. F. R. Raines, The Rectors of Manchester and the Wardens of the Collegiate Church, *The Chetham Society*, 1885, pt.II, p.172.

6. Richard Hartley died of smallpox at Clayton's school in 1739.

7. It must be said that Devis' representation of the school does not bear the remotest resemblance to the original brick building which stood at the corner of Gravel Lane, Greengate, Salford, and an illustration of which is reproduced opp. p.266, in the volume referred to in note 1.

8. A similar arrangement of scientific instruments placed high on a shelf appears in an engraving 'The FIRST lecture in EXPERIMENTAL PHILOSOPHY' in *The Universal Magazine* of 1748.

PROVENANCE: Presumably in the Byrom family since painted; by descent to Miss Eleonora Atherton of Byrom, Kersall Cell and Manchester; on her death 1870 willed to her godson Edward Vigor Fox (who adopted the name Byrom to qualify for the inheritance); thence by descent to his great-granddaughter Rose Effie Jerardine Eden, who gave the picture to Manchester Grammar School 1946–47, a cousin of hers being the wife of Lord James Rusholme, High Master of the School 1945–61. Sold by the School at Christie's, 21 March 1975 (58, ill.); bt. Peters; Paul Anstee; bt. (Grant-in-Aid), Tate Gallery, 1980.

REFERENCES: Richard Parkinson (ed.), 'The Private Journal and Literary Remains of John Byrom' in *The Chetham Society*, 1855, I, ii, p.509, no.1; Rev. F. R. Raines, 'The Rectors of Manchester and the Wardens of the Collegiate Church' in *The Chetham Society* 1885, pt.II, p.172, and 'The Fellows of Manchester' in *ditto*, 1891, pt.II, p.257, 266; 'The Poems of John Byrom', pt.I, vol.I, pp.151–155; *Dictionary of National Biography*, 1908, for Clayton and Byrom; A. A. Mumford, *Manchester Grammar School 1515–1919*, Longman's, 1919, pp.160–62, 174, repr.; Frank Davis 'A School for Jacobites' in *Country Life*, 24 April 1975, repr. p.1038; John H. Bell, 'Breaking-up Day at Dr. Clayton's School,

Salford' in *Ulula* (Manchester Grammar School Magazine), No.549, September 1976, pp.91–92, repr.; Ellen D'Oench 'Arthur Devis, Master of the Georgian Conversation Piece,' Yale Doctoral Thesis, 1979, Cat, no.33,, pp.298–99; and catalogue of Devis exhibition, Yale, 1980, no.33.

10. John Bacon and his Family
c. 1742–43
Canvas, 30⅛ × 51⅝ in.
Yale Center for British Art, Paul Mellon Collection, New Haven, Connecticut, U.S.A.

This magnificent painting with its carefully measured proportions and exquisitely-handled detail is the perfect vehicle for expressing the modes and manners of polite society in Hanoverian London.

The family of John Bacon gather together in an elegant drawing room evoking an image of marital contentment as it might be described in the pages of a Richardson novel. John Bacon himself adopts a severity of demeanour befitting a learned academic. His son, John William, holds a flute to demonstrate his musical accomplishments, while his two other children, Charles and Cathérine, quietly amuse themselves building a house of cards. Centrally placed is his wife, Catherine, who caresses their youngest daughter, Dorothy, with maternal affection.

Ellen G. D'Oench[1] has drawn attention to the presence in the room of a reflecting telescope, transit quadrant, and other scientific instruments to indicate Bacon's interests as a Fellow of the Royal Society. The medallion portraits of John Milton, Alexander Pope, Sir Francis Bacon, and Isaac Newton[2] are no doubt included to show a wider interest in poetry and philosophy.

Although ostentatious to 20th century eyes, the Palladian drawing room would at the time have been regarded as a model of restraint and refinement in keeping with the philosophy of the Whig aristocracy.

1. See D'Oench, Cat. 6, for a discussion on this painting.

2. For further information on the medallion portraits see John Reily and W. K. Wimsatt, 'Supplement to the Portraits of Alexander Pope,' *Evidence in Literary Scholarship, Essays in Memory of James Marshall Osborn*, Ed. R. Wellek and A. Ribeiro, Oxford, 1979, pp.150–51.

PROVENANCE: By descent from John Bacon to his grandson, John Bacon; with his daughter, Emily Bacon Grey, who bequeathed it to her 2nd cousin, Sir Percy Loraine, Bt. in 1918; acquired from an unknown owner by Spink & Son; bt. Paul Mellon, 1968.

EXHIBITED: Yale Center for British Art, *The Conversation Piece: Arthur Devis and His Contemporaries*, New Haven, 1980, Cat. 6, repr.

REFERENCES: See note 2.

11. Roger Hesketh and his Family, of Rossall, Lancashire   c. 1742–43   P

Canvas, 40 × 50 in.
Roger Fleetwood Hesketh, Lancashire

In this and the following catalogue entry[1] architectural features are so alike as to rule out any actual association between the sitters and their surroundings. When this picture was painted, Roger Hesketh owned country houses in three estates in Lancashire – Rossall Hall near Fleetwood, Meols Hall near what was to be Southport, and Tulketh Hall near Preston. In the 1740s he is known to have been resident in Tulketh Hall,[2] an ancient building with crenellated turrets, which did not have a remote resemblance to the monumental interior painted by Devis.

Roger Hesketh (1711–91) inherited his father's estates when he was twelve years old. In 1733 he married Margaret, daughter of Edward Fleetwood of Rossall, by whom he had a son, Fleetwood, and a daughter, Sarah. He was admitted as a freeman of the borough of Preston in 1737, and in 1742 played a prominent rôle in the Guild Merchant celebrations. Devis also was in Preston in 1742 to renew his own freedom, and it is reasonable to assume that he was commissioned to paint this portrait and several others at that time.

Devis must have known Roger Hesketh to be a man of scientific tastes, and has made reference to this by including a globe in the foreground and a telescope in the far room. Such interests must have remained with him all his life, for a marble monument to him in Churchtown Church, North Meols, is decorated with a globe, quadrant and books.

1. Although it is not known for whom Cat. 12, *Children in an Interior* was painted, no link with the Hesketh family can be found.

2. Preston Borough archives, MS Guild Order Book, p.731, *"Roger Hesketh late of Meols now of Preston admitted a ffree (man) Mon. Aug. 1, 1737 under mayoralty of Henry Farington."*

PROVENANCE: By descent to the present owner.

EXHIBITED: Southport, Atkinson Art Gallery, *Festival of Britain, Exhibition of Local Art Treasures* 1951 (150), repr.; Manchester, City Art Gallery,

Exhibition of Works from Private Collections in the West of England and North Wales, 1960 (135); Yale Center for British Art, *The Conversation Piece: Arthur Devis and His Contemporaries,* New Haven, 1980, Cat. 7, repr.

REFERENCES: Pavière (66); D'Oench, Cat. 7; Liverpool Daily Post, *Country Heritage,* 1951, p.70; John Cornforth, 'Meols Hall, Lancashire I' *Country Life* 153, January 25, 1973, p.209, repr. pl.8.

12. Children in an Interior   c. 1742–43

Canvas, 39 × 49¾ in.
Yale Center for British Art, Paul Mellon Collection, New Haven, Connecticut, U.S.A.

It is not known for whom Devis executed this important commission, but its provenance suggests someone living in the area of Dorset.[1]

Although English in its reserve, this charming conversation piece owes something to the fancy pictures popularised at the time by artists such as Philip Mercier.[2] The eldest girl seated at the table adopts a pose in keeping with that of mistress of the house, while the boy with the kite takes up a stance in imitation of his father. One of the children is building a house of cards, a recurring subject in anecdotal paintings of the period. A particularly attractive feature is the meticulous and studied brushwork to indicate delicate details – the texture of the work basket, the light and shadow of the house of cards, and the crispness of the trimmings on the boy's waistcoat.

Ellen D'Oench has drawn attention to the remarkable similarity between the interior and that of the painting of the Hesketh family[3] (Cat. 11), in which even the shadow falls across the floor at the same angle. The picture is in effect a stage-set with figures acting their parts in an interior based on motifs derived from architectural pattern books available at the time.[4]

1. It was owned by Mr. and Mrs. Eric Bullivant of Anderson Manor, Dorset.

2. See John Ingamells and Robert Raines, 'A Catalogue of the Paintings, Drawings and Etchings of Philip Mercier,' *Walpole Society,* 42, 1976–78, pp.1–70, with repr.

3. D'Oench, Cat. 7, 8.

4. See *The Gentleman's and Builder's Repository,* with designs by E. Hoppus, engraved by B. Cole, London, 1738, pl.LXVIII, and LXXIII for very similar shields to the one on the left of the archway.

PROVENANCE: Mr. and Mrs. Eric Bullivant of Anderson Manor, Dorset; Sotheby's, July 17, 1974 (100) as *The Cholmondeley Children*; bt. Richard Green Galleries; bt. private collector; purchased by the Yale Center for British Art, 1978.

EXHIBITED: Yale Center for British Art, *The Conversation Piece: Arthur Devis and His Contemporaries*, New Haven, 1980 (8) repr.

REFERENCES: Catalogue of the above exhibition, Cat. 7, 8.

13. Robert Gwillym, of Atherton, and his Family   c. 1745–46

Canvas, 39⅝ × 50 in.
Yale Center for British Art, Paul Mellon Collection, New Haven, Connecticut, U.S.A.

Formerly known as *Robert Vernon Atherton and his Family*, this picture was renamed *Robert Gwillym, of Atherton, and his Family* following researches by Nancy Pressly[1] at Hereford Records Office.

Robert Gwillym is shown here standing with his father, Robert Gwillym (1692–1750), of the parish of St. Nicholas, Hereford. To the right his wife, Elizabeth, daughter of Richard Atherton (1700–1726) of Atherton, sits with their four surviving children, Robert Vernon (1741–83),[2] Elizabeth Goldsmith, Jane, and William. Pressly suggested that the man on the right is William (died 1749), one of Robert Gwillym's three brothers. Ellen D'Oench, correctly dating the picture earlier, suggests it could be one of his other brothers, Thomas or Charles, both of whom died in 1748. Of the brothers it is much more likely to be Charles, who lived at nearby Chowbent, and who bequeathed the major part of his estate to Robert and Elizabeth when he died in 1748. Devis was in Lancashire in 1742 to renew his freeman's rights at the Preston Guild Merchant, and again c. 1745–46, when he was paid £6.15s for painting a picture of Walton School for Sir Henry Hoghton. Since the eldest surviving son of the couple, Robert Vernon, was only born in 1741, this picture probably dates from the beginning of 1746.

This raises an interesting question as to whether Atherton Hall as it appears in the painting is correct in its architectural details.[3] It is said to have been completed in 1743,[4] but comparison of its façade as it is engraved in Colen Campbell's *Vitruvius Britannicus* (London, 1725, vol.3, pl.89) and as it is shown here indicates that the building had not been completed by that date. This is confirmed by a letter written on June 7, 1754 by Dr. Richard Pococke[5] in which he describes how he "came in

the road to Legh and struck out of it to see New hall, a fine seat with large offices built by Mr. Atherton, who married his daughter to Mr. Guillaume, of Herefordshire, who lives here, but the house is not entirely finished, nor kept in good order; the front is adorned with Ionick-fluted pillars and pilasters, and there is a handsome avenue to it from Legh." The existence of a drawing executed by William Latham,[6] September 16, 1823 suggests, however, that William Wakefield's original plans for four engaged columns surmounted by a pediment were realised at some later date.

1. See exhibition catalogue *The Pursuit of Happiness, a View of Life in Georgian England*, Yale Center for British Art, New Haven, 1977 (135). Cat. by Edward Nygren, J. H. Plumb, and Nancy Pressly.

2. Robert Vernon assumed the name Atherton by Royal Warrant in 1779.

3. See D'Oench, Cat. 15, and Kerry Downes. *English Baroque Architecture* (London, 1966), p.92, for further reference.

4. See John Lunn, *Atherton, Lancashire: A Manorial, Social and Industrial History*, Atherton, 1971, p.99.

5. See *The Travels through England of Dr. Richard Pococke, during 1750, 1751, and Later Years*. Ed. James J. Cartwright, Camden Society, vol.2, 1889, pp.8, 9.

6. See Lunn, repr. opp. p.154.

PROVENANCE: By descent from Henrietta Maria, daughter of Robert Vernon Atherton, to the family of Lord Lilford of Lilford Hall, Northamptonshire, 1961; purchased by Sabin Galleries, London, from whom acquired by Paul Mellon.

EXHIBITED: Richmond, Virginia Museum of Fine Arts, *Painting in England, 1700–1850, from the Collection of Mr. and Mrs. Paul Mellon*, 1963 (227), repr. pl.84; R.A. *Painting in England, 1700–1850, from the collection of Mr. and Mrs. Paul Mellon*, 1964–65 (204), repr. on cover. As *Robert Vernon Atherton and his Family*, in the above exhibitions; New Haven, Yale Center for British Art, *The Pursuit of Happiness, a View of Life in Georgian England*, 1977 (135), repr.; New Haven, Yale Center for British Art, *Country Houses in Great Britain*, 1979–80 (16); New Haven, Yale Center for British Art, *The Conversation Piece: Arthur Devis and His Contemporaries*, 1980 (15), repr.

REFERENCES: D'Oench (15), repr.; John Baskett, 'Painting in England, 1700–1850,' *Connoisseur* 153 (June 1963), p.101; *Time* 82 (July 5, 1963), p.62; *Life* 55 (Aug. 9, 1963), repr. p.49; 'Collectors' Questions', *Country Life* 134 (Sept. 5, 1963), repr. p.536, an answer to a query from Mary Atherton Mounthorn giving the name of the house as

Atherton Hall; John Cornforth. 'The Informality of English Painting,' *Country Life Annual* (1965), repr. p.18; Geoffrey Beard, *Georgian Craftsmen and Their Work,* London, 1966, p.102, repr. pl.11; Kerry Downes, *English Baroque Architecture,* London 1966, p.92; Christopher Neve, 'Arthur Devis, a Minor English Master,' *Country Life Annual* (1972), repr. p.44; Mario Praz, *Conversation Pieces: A Survey of the Informal Group Portrait in Europe and America,* Pennsylvania, 1971, p.138, repr. pl.96; John Harris, *The Artist and the Country House: A History of Country House and Garden View Painting in Britain, 1550–1850,* London, 1979 (231); John Lunn, *Atherton, Lancashire: A Manorial, Social and Industrial History,* Atherton, 1971, ref. to Atherton House; *The Travels through England of Dr. Richard Pococke, during 1750, 1751, and Later Years,* Ed. James J. Cartwright, Camden Society, vol.2, 1889, pp.8, 9.

14. William Atherton and his Wife, Lucy, of Preston, Lancashire   c. 1742–44

Canvas, 36¼ × 50 in.   *NPG*
Merseyside County Council (Walker Art Gallery, Liverpool)

William Atherton is shown here with his wife in a spacious apartment of a house which stands in a landscape garden. In truth, he lived in a house overlooking Preston Market Square on a site now occupied by the Harris Street corner of the Harris Museum and Art Gallery. When this picture was painted, the land in the immediate vicinity comprised a network of narrow passages leading through butchers' shops and slaughter-houses. This contrast of myth and reality highlights a conceit in which some of Devis' patrons were willing participants in a 'deception' which would have been obvious to those who knew them.[1] Ellen D'Oench has suggested that the interior is partially accurate with the inclusion of a cabinet against the wall on the right which is similar to those made by the Lancashire craftsman, Gillow, and which is not to be found in any other painting by Devis.

William Atherton was a wealthy Preston woollen draper. He took an active part in governing the town from 1724, when he was elected bailiff, until his death in 1745. He was elected to the Town Council in 1728, one year before Anthony Devis, Arthur's father, assumed the same office.[2] In 1731 he became an Alderman of the borough, and in 1732–33 and 1738–39 served as Mayor. However, his most powerful appointment was as a Steward of the Guild Merchant of 1742, in which rôle he and three other Council members had the authority to admit any person as a Free-Inn-Burgess or Foreign Burgess of Preston without further consultation. Since a freeman's privileges included

the right to vote in parliamentary elections, he effectively was able to ensure the re-election of the "tiresome Jacobite lawyer," Nicholas Fazackerley (Cat. 52).

1. Devis' paintings are often used in a social historical context to illustrate life in the eighteenth century, but on the evidence supplied by this portrait they can be quite misleading. Whilst there are several paintings by him illustrating known topographical scenes (See Cat. 44), there are virtually no illustrations of interiors which can be identified specifically with the sitters. A notable exception to this is the portrait of *Sir Roger Newdigate in his Library at Arbury Hall, Warwickshire,* (Cat. 38).

2. The two must have known each other well. As councilmen they consistently attended Council and Court Leet meetings together over a period of fourteen years.

PROVENANCE: By descent on her mother's side to Francis Eliza Wynne-Griffith, later Lady Daresbury; purchased from her by the Walker Art Gallery, 1940.

EXHIBITED: London, 25 Park Lane, *Loan Exhibition of English Conversation Pieces of the Eighteenth Century,* 1930 (94); Preston, *Lancashire Art,* 1937 (23); London, National Gallery, *Some Acquisitions of the Walker Art Gallery, 1935–45,* 1945 (4); Liverpool, Walker Art Gallery, *Twenty Portraits,* 1947 (1), repr.; Lisbon, British Council, 1949 (14); Hamburg, British Council, 1949–50 (36); Liverpool, Walker Art Gallery, *Painting and Sculpture in England, 1700–1750,* 1958 (7); London, Kenwood, Iveagh Bequest, *The Conversation Piece in Georgian England,* 1965 (11); New Haven, Yale Center for British Art, *The Conversation Piece: Arthur Devis and His Contemporaries,* 1980 (11).

REFERENCES: Pavière (5), repr. pl.25; D'Oench, Cat. 11; G. C. Williamson, *English Conversation Pictures of the Eighteenth and Nineteenth Centuries,* London, 1931, p.12, repr. pl.XXX; C. H. Collins Baker, 'Devis, Scott, and Highmore,' *Antiques 67,* (January 1955), pp.41–47; John Cornforth, 'Intimacy and the Conversation Piece,' *Country Life* 138 (July 1, 1965), p.13; *The Times,* June 18, 1965, repr. p.15; R. J. Charleston, 'Porcelain as Room Decoration in Eighteenth-Century England,' *Antiques* 96 (December 1969), repr. p.897; Mario Praz, *Conversation Pieces: A Survey of the Informal Group Portrait in Europe and America,* Pennsylvania, 1971, p.162, repr. pl.312; David Piper, ed., *The Genius of British Painting,* N.Y., 1975, repr. p.158; William Gaunt, *The Great Century of British Painting: Hogarth to Turner,* Oxford, 1978, repr. pl.39.

15. The Rev. Streynsham Master and his Wife, of Croston, Lancashire   1742–44

Canvas, 32½ × 39½ in.
Private Collection

Following his short-lived phase of painting monumental interiors, Devis here continues a trend, already apparent in the previous catalogue entry, towards a more intimate architectural scale and a less dramatic use of light. This is also accompanied by the development of a more static composition consisting of strong horizontals and verticals.[1]

The painting also reflects the changing taste of the period by including a fine ormolu clock on a rococo side table. There is the possibility that they were the personal possessions of the Rev. Master, and this is made more plausible because Devis must have visited Croston to draw the church which is visible through the window. However, the left side of the composition is almost identical to that in the portrait of *William Atherton and his Wife Lucy* (Cat. 14).

The Rev. Streynsham Master, Vicar of Croston, is shown here seated with his wife. Beyond are portraits of his brother and sister. Devis may have been commissioned to paint the portrait when he was in Preston to attend the Guild Merchant ceremony held in September 1742. Master had been enrolled as a Free-Inn-Burgess of the town in November 1740, and would also have been in Preston in 1742 to have this confirmed.

1. Devis considerably reduces the dramatic effect so apparent in *Roger Hesketh and his Family, of Rossall, Lancashire* (Cat. 11), and *Children in an Interior* (Cat. 12) by substituting the strong diagonal shadow for one less pronounced and running horizontally across the picture plane.

PROVENANCE: W. S. Curtis, Newton Abbot, 1937; C. Marshall Spink; bt. by a private collector; by descent to the present owner.

EXHIBITED: Preston, *Lancashire Art*, 1937 (18); Winchester College and Southampton Art Gallery, *Old Masters from Hampshire Houses*, 1955.

REFERENCES: *Country Life* 61 (March 13, 1937), repr. pl.lx; *The Sphere* 148 (March 20, 1937), p.451, repr.; *Illustrated London News* 190 (March 20, 1937), p.503, repr.; *The Saturday Book* (1952), repr.; *Illustrated London News* (July 2, 1955), repr.

16. Gentleman and Lady in a Landscape c. 1747–49

Signed and dated 174(?)
Canvas, 28 × 36 in.
The National Trust, Wimpole Hall, Arrington, Cambridgeshire

This painting of an unknown gentleman and lady was known for many years under the romantic title of *Horace Walpole presenting Kitty Clive with a Piece of Honeysuckle.*[1] It has also been suggested that the gentleman is either the Hon. Thomas Walpole, or his brother, Richard, and that the lady is a member of the family of Sir Joshua Vanneck of Roehampton House, Putney.[2]

Ellen D'Oench has noted the discovery of a '4' in the third digit of the date, and concludes from the costume of the figures that the painting was executed in the late 1740s.[3]

A pronounced feature of some of Devis' earlier paintings is the lack of tonal contrast in landscapes and interiors. It is clearly to be observed in this painting in which the highlights on the two figures are much brighter than the clouds in the sky and details of foliage in the foreground.

1. It is so described in Sitwell, and G. C. Williamson. See References.

2. See Pavière (45).

3. Pavière read the date as 1767. See D'Oench, list 242.

PROVENANCE: Lady Margaret Douglas, 1936; Sotheby's, July 3, 1940 (116), repr.; bt. Permain; Wimpole Hall, Arrington; National Trust, Wimpole Hall.

EXHIBITED: London, *English Conversation Pieces*, 1930 (85), repr.

REFERENCES: Pavière (45); D'Oench, list 242; G. C. Williamson, *English Conversation Pieces*, London, 1931, p.11, pl.31; Sacheverell Sitwell, *Conversation Pieces*, London, 1936, p.51, pl.56.

17. The Duet   1749

Signed and dated
Canvas, 45½ × 40¾ in.
Victoria and Albert Museum, London

When this picture was painted the ability to play a musical instrument was regarded as a desirable accomplishment in most circles of polite society. Visitors to Bath who wished to attend the fashionable breakfast concerts were reminded that "Persons of rank and fortune, who can perform, are admitted into the orchestra, and find a pleasure in joining with the performers."[1] However, no less an authority on polite behaviour than Lord Chesterfield regarded the practicalities of music-making with disdain — "If you love music, hear it; go to operas, concerts, and pay fiddlers to play to you; but I insist upon your neither piping nor fiddling yourself. It puts a gentleman in a very frivolous, contemptible light; brings him into a great deal of bad company; and takes up a great deal of time, which might be much better employed. Few things would mortify me more, than to see you bearing a part in a concert, with a fiddle under your chin or a pipe in your mouth."[2]

A characteristic feature of Devis' method of painting, of which this is a good example, is the way in which he skilfully delineates all objects, regardless of their relative importance in the picture. Here it will be seen that equal emphasis has been given to the construction of the violin and to the texture of the mahogany of the harpsichord, as it has to the figures themselves.

Almost certainly the design of the Palladian window has been taken from one of the numerous architectural pattern books available at the time.[3]

1. See 'Rules to be observed at Bath' in Oliver Goldsmith's *Life of Richard Nash* 1762, a transcription of which is in, David Daiches and John Flower, *Literary Landscapes of the British Isles, A Narrative Atlas,* Paddington Press, 1979, p.97.

2. Letter of the Earl of Chesterfield to his Son, London, April 19, O.S. 1749.

3. See a similar Venetian window of the Ionic order in Batty Langley, *The City and Country Builder's and Workman's Treasury of Designs,* pl.LIII, London, 1745.

PROVENANCE: Hornsby-Drake Sale as *The Love Song* (Cecil Fane de Salis, Henley-on-Thames, collection) Christie's, March 11, 1932; bt. Gooden and Fox; E. E. Cook; bequeathed to National Art Collections Fund and acquired by the Victoria and Albert Museum in 1955.

EXHIBITED: Yale Center for British Art, *The Conversation Piece: Arthur Devis and His Contemporaries,* New Haven, 1980 (22) repr.

REFERENCES: Pavière (103); Sacheverell Sitwell, The World of Arthur Devis, *Saturday Book,* 12, 1952, p.94 repr.; *Connoisseur,* 136, The Ernest Cook Bequest to the National Art Collections Fund, repr., Sept. 1955; R. Russell, *Early Keyboard Instruments,* London, 1959, repr. on book jacket; D'Oench, Cat. 22, repr.

18. Robert Dashwood and his Wife, Anne, of Stamford Park, Nottinghamshire 1750

Signed and dated   P
Canvas, 44 × 38 in.
Private Collection

A comparison of this portrait of Mr. and Mrs. Dashwood with another work, *'Mr. and Mrs. Bull, of Ongar, Essex,'* affords an interesting insight into the method Devis employed in constructing his compositions. Both paintings are close versions of each other with the figures adopting almost identical poses and positions, and the architectural interior being exactly the same. There are minor changes which the artist probably made to suit the temperaments of his sitters. In the painting of Mr. and Mrs. Bull a row of oriental ceramics decorates the mantelpiece, and on the floor is a Persian carpet. Here, however, the ceramics have been replaced by a single newspaper and the carpet has vanished from the floor. In addition, the chairs are somewhat different, as are the costumes on the figures. The close parallel between the two works, one painted three years after the other, prompts the question as to whether Devis prepared several canvases with the same interior on which to superimpose the faces of different sitters;[2] and also, with two canvases of a similar size, whether he adopted a sliding scale of charges for the extra work involved in adding an elaborately-patterned carpet and a row of ceramics to one of the pictures.

Robert Dashwood was a grandson of Sir Robert Dashwood, 1st Bt., M.P., through a third surviving son, Richard. His wife, Anne, was the daughter and co-heir of Francis Lewes of Stamford, Nottinghamshire. Little is known of Robert Dashwood's politics, but his cousin Sir James Dashwood, of Kirtlington Park, Oxfordshire, represented his county as a Tory in Parliament (1740–54, 1761–68) and is said to have been "strongly tainted with Jacobitism".[3]

1. There is a colour reproduction of *'Mr. and Mrs. Bull, of Ongar, Essex'* in D'Oench, Cat 19.

2. Devis no doubt ensured that in such cases his sitters would live far enough apart to make it unlikely that they would see each other's paintings. Or so one would hope!

3. Romney Sedgwick, *The History of Parliament, The House of Commons, 1715–54* (H.M.S.O. London 1970), vol.1, p.605.

PROVENANCE: By descent to N. C. C. Giradot; Sotheby's, July 1975; bt. by the present owner.

EXHIBITED: Long term loan to the Harris Museum and Art Gallery, Preston, 1973–75.

REFERENCES: D'Oench, list 45, and Cat. 19.

19. Louis Combrune, of Lothbury 1745

Signed and dated
Panel, 24 × 16½ in.
Private Collection

Although Louis Combrune had no apparent association with Preston, his name appears on a list of nobility and gentry who dined with the mayor during the celebrations of the Preston Guild Merchant of 1762.[1] Since he was not a freeman of the borough, his presence suggests that he was representing the Brewers' Company, of which he was a member, in one of the principal and most ancient ceremonies of the Guild, the Trades Procession.

Here he is shown wearing a brown coat over a gold-embroidered white satin waistcoat, and black breeches. He holds an opened letter in his hand, and adopts a characteristic cross-legged stance much favoured by Devis (Cat. 20).

In a deliberate distortion of the rules of perspective, the artist has adjusted the receding lines of the floor to converge on the left of the picture, which has the effect of concentrating the attention of the viewer on the hand holding the letter. This, together with the sails of a ship partially glimpsed through the window to the right, must relate to an unknown event in the life of Louis Combrune, which he required Devis to record.

Little is known of his life, but he is known to have married Helen, daughter of Thomas (1684–1775) and Eleanor (d. 1754) Gardnor, of Hampstead, London, and to have died in 1764.

The painting is related to two portrait groups with the same provenance. The first[2] shows members of the Gardnor family gathered around a harpsichord and a tripod table in a wooded landscape. The second[3] is a close copy of the first, with the portrait of Louis Combrune added to the right-hand side of the picture. Presumably this was painted at the time of Helen Gardnor's marriage.

1. W. A. Abram, *Memorials of the Preston Guilds*, 1882, p.95.

2. Sotheby's, March 18, 1964 (99) repr.

3. Sotheby's, March 25, 1975 (56) repr.

PROVENANCE: Mrs. Dorothy Ireland; Sotheby's, March 18, 1964; bt. for the present owner.

20. Wrightson Mundy, of Osbaston, Leicestershire, and Markeaton, Derbyshire 1749
P

Signed and dated
Canvas, 29 × 24 in.
Private Collection

Wrightson Mundy (c. 1712–62) was the first son of Francis Mundy of Osbaston, and Anne, daughter of Sir John Noel, 4th Bt., of Kirkby Mallory, Leicestershire. He was educated at Winchester and Pembroke College, Cambridge. He became High-Sheriff of Derbyshire in 1737, and was elected member of Parliament for Leicestershire in 1747.

Like his father, he was regarded as a keen Jacobite, and in the year in which this portrait was painted he was described by Lord Egmont[1] as "a young man reputed a thorough Jacobite. He is talked up among the Tories as the most promising man of the whole party but has never spoken yet." However, his promising parliamentary career slipped away with his ill-health, and he did not stand for re-election in 1754.

This is one of five portraits commissioned by John Arden of Harden Hall, Tarporley, Cheshire, the subjects of which, according to family tradition, were close friends of his when he was studying at Pembroke College in 1731. The sitters represented in the other portraits were the Rev. Sir William Bunbury, of Mildenhall, Suffolk, William Chaworth of Annesley, Nottinghamshire, and William Trollope of Pembroke College, Cambridge. There must, however, be another association – the Chaworth and Mundy families were related to each other through the Pole family of Derbyshire, and Wrightson Mundy's wife, Anne, was the niece of Elizabeth, daughter of Sir Thomas Trollope of Casewick, Lincolnshire. Wrightson Mundy also had an association with Preston, in that he was a first cousin once removed to Mary, daughter of Gilbert Mundy of Shipley Hall, Derbyshire, and wife of Thomas Molyneux, a wealthy merchant who lived in Fishergate, Preston. Thomas Molyneux was an ardent Whig, and this may well have been a factor in the acrimony between the two families which arose over the settlement of Gilbert Mundy's estate on his death in 1716.[2]

This portrait, which is so characteristic of Devis' small whole-lengths, shows Wrightson Mundy wearing a grey suit over a white waistcoat, and a black tricorn hat. He leans against an oak tree, holding a silver pen and a half-completed letter in his right hand. The landscape background is apparently fanciful, and has no topographical relationship to the Mundy family estates in Derbyshire. This is confirmed by the existence of a close version of the painting, in which the landscape background has small but significant modifications.

1. Romney Sedgwick, *The History of Parliament, The House of Commons, 1715–54,* (H.M.S.O. London, 1970), vol.2, pp.280–81.

2. MS diary of Mary Molyneux, wife of Thomas Molyneux of Preston, and daughter of Gilbert Mundy, 1716–39, Harris Museum and Art Gallery, Preston.

PROVENANCE: John Arden of Harden Hall, Tarporley, Cheshire; by descent to Desmond O'Brien of Arden; Sotheby's, March 10, 1965 (109); acquired by the present owner.

REFERENCES: D'Oench, list 116.

21. Thomas Starkie, of Frenchwood House, Preston   1749   P

Signed and dated
Canvas, 30 × 25 in.
Harris Museum and Art Gallery, Preston

Thomas Starkie, a Preston solicitor, was the son of Nicholas Starkie, barrister-at-law, and Attorney-General of the County Palatine. Both he and his brother Edmund were influential members of the Town Council and therefore well placed to promote their keen Jacobite sympathies. It is said that when Prince Charles Edward marched through Preston with his Highlanders in 1745 he lodged at the house of Thomas' brother, Edmund.[1]

Thomas Starkie was elected mayor of Preston in 1754. He lived at Frenchwood House which he had had built circa 1730. Here he is shown seated beneath an oak tree on the south side of the house, overlooking the Ribble valley. To the left, on a steep incline, is St. Leonard's Church, Walton-le-Dale, with Hoghton Tower crowning the summit of a hill in the distance. There has been some controversy as to whether the painting may be regarded as being of Thomas Starkie on the basis of the landscape background.[2] However, while it is true that Devis often includes river scenes in his paintings, the precise configuration of river, church, and Hoghton Tower on its characteristically-shaped hill, as they appear from Frenchwood House, which still exists, is more than coincidence would allow. Perhaps the only freedom Devis allowed himself was in the painting of the landscape in the immediate foreground, which is common to many of his works.

Another painting formerly regarded as a portrait of *Thomas Starkie and his Wife*[3] can not sustain an identification with the Starkie family on the grounds of the landscape background alone.

1. See *The Private Journal and Literary Remains of John Byrom,* Chetham Society, 1855, p.388.

2. See D'Oench, list 226.

3. See D'Oench, list 244, (phot. Cooper 706099).

PROVENANCE: Purchased from Rembrandt Gallery, London, by Harris Museum and Art Gallery, 1936.

EXHIBITED: Rembrandt Gallery, London, *Conversation Pieces and small Portraits,* 1936 (9).

REFERENCES: Pavière, *Walpole Society,* vol.25, pl.42a; D'Oench, list 226.

22. Miss Sarah Tyssen, of Hackney, Middlesex   1748   P

Signed and dated indistinctly
Canvas, 19½ × 13½ in.
Private Collection

The date of the painting, often given as 1743, is almost certainly 1748. A late nineteenth-century inscription on the reverse suggests that the young lady is Sarah Tyssen, eldest daughter of Samuel Tyssen (1698–1748) of Hackney, Middlesex, a wealthy man with a sugar plantation in Antigua, and Mrs. Sarah Littell, widow of John Eden Littell, of the Worshipful Company of Salters. In 1752 she married Richard Bodicott, a city merchant of Homerton, Hackney, Middlesex. Apparently, both she and her half-sister, Miss Littell, were engaged to be married to Richard Bodicott. A further inscription on the reverse "Miss Little, to whom Mr. Bodicott was engaged but not married to her" puts some doubt on the identity of the portrait. However, it could just mean that Sarah Tyssen was engaged but not yet married.[1] It is also relevant that the portrait was owned by her direct descendants.

Sarah Tyssen, standing in a garden near an obelisk, wears an open robe, a quilted blue petticoat, and a transparent apron. On her head she wears a round-eared cap and carries a bergère hat. The painting also shows to advantage the stiff cone shape of the stays under the bodice.

1. See D'Oench, list 105 and 11 for a discussion on this. The inscription reads *This picture left by Rev. John Yelloty to his nephew in March 1892 his nephew Rev. Robert Sackling, St. Albans, Holborn; and Sarah wife of John Eden Littell of Ballingdon Hall and daughter of Solomon Hougham and Mildred his wife, he died Jan. 1728. buried Sudbury Suffolk married in 1730 Samuel Tyssen of Hackney died in 1778 Sarah and Samuel Tyssen's eldest daughter in 1752 Richard Bodicott from whom we are directly descended. Mary Sackling.*

23. Lady in a Blue Dress   c. 1748
Canvas, 22 × 15½ in.
Private Collection

This small whole-length portrait is a masterly example of that naive charm so often to be found in Devis' paintings. The unknown woman stands erect, a model of genteel deportment. Her poise and demeanour enable her to wear a comparatively simple blue dress to great effect. The important part played by sensibility of the mind in a well-dressed person was recognised by *The Tatler*[1] in a description so appropriate to this painting — "There is such a composure in her looks, and propriety in her dress, that you would think it impossible she should change the garb you one day see her in for anything so becoming, till you next day see her in another. There is no other mystery in this, but that however she is apparelled, she is herself the same: for there is so immediate a relation between our thoughts and gestures, that a woman must think well to look well."

Particularly fine is the skilful placing of the figure against the geometric shapes comprising the interior of the room, as also is the contrast of the subtle shades of blue in the costume with the red-brown carpet and background of ochre and dark blue.

1. *The Tatler*, August 16, 1710, No. 212.

24. Lucy Watson (later Mrs. John Thornton of Clapham)   c. 1749   P
Indistinctly signed
Canvas, 24 × 16 in.
Trustees of R. J. Meade-Fetherstonhaugh, decd., on loan to Uppark

In this charming whole-length portrait, executed with an attention to detail worthy of a miniature painter, Devis has invested his sitter with the fragile grace and delicately affected pose of a porcelain figure. Rather than art being judged as a mirror of nature, here we see reality itself trans-formed by the social etiquette of the time.

Lucy Watson wears a magnificent pink open robe, blue petticoat over an oblong hoop, elbow-sleeves with pleated cuffs, and a neckerchief over her bosom. On her head is a small round-eared cap, a type popular at the time.

The interior with slight variations is common to many other small whole-length portraits executed by Devis.

25. Sir James Burrow, of Starborough Castle, Lingfield, Surrey   1749   P
Signed and dated
Canvas, 24 × 16½ in.
Private Collection

Typical of many small whole-lengths executed by Devis throughout his career, this portrait shows Sir James Burrow[1] wearing a gold-trimmed blue coat, white satin waistcoat, and black breeches, seated under an oak tree in a romantic coastal landscape. Whilst it is more than likely that it was painted to hang at Starborough Castle, an identical version was commissioned in the same year by Sir Matthew Fetherstonhaugh[2] of Uppark, West Sussex. If the latter is the original painting, then perhaps the distant prospect of the sea is an allusion to the situation of Uppark near the south coast.

Sir James Burrow (1701-82) was the son of Thomas Burrow of Clapham, Surrey. In 1725 he was called to the bar at the Inner Temple, and in later years held high offices there. In 1733 he obtained the post of Master of the Crown Office which he retained throughout his life. Particularly interesting is his fellowship of the Royal Society[3] (1737) and of the Society of Antiquaries (1741), for in these circles he must first have become acquainted with several of Devis' patrons including Sir Matthew Fetherstonhaugh, members of the Lethieullier family (Cat. 26), and also John Byrom (Cat. 9).

1. Two other portraits of Sir James Burrow were commissioned from Devis. One of these is in a private collection in Wales. The other, depicting Sir James as Master of the Crown Office, is now lost, and known only from a line engraving dated 1780 by James Basire. The size of the engraving (19¼ × 14⅛ in.) is common to many small portraits by Devis and it is probable that it is a faithful facsimile of the original painting. See D'Oench, list 22, 23, 24.

2. Following his succession to his father's vast estates in Essex, Hertfordshire, Middlesex, and the City of London, in 1746, Sir Matthew Fetherstonhaugh commissioned Devis in the same year, to paint his portrait as a small whole-length. He must have been pleased with it for in the following years Devis painted eleven other portraits of a similar size. The version of this painting still hangs with seven others at Uppark.

3. Sir James was a man of great academic accomplishments. Apart from numerous legal publications, he also contributed five papers on earthquakes to the Philosophical Transactions of the Royal Society.

PROVENANCE: Viscountess Cowdray; by descent to the present owner.

26. William Wallis Lethieullier (called Boy Fishing)   c. 1749   *P*

Signed and indistinctly dated
Canvas, 24 × 16 in.
Trustees of R. J. Meade-Fetherstonhaugh, decd., on loan to Uppark

This charming portrait of a youth fishing on the banks of a river is the nearest Devis' art approaches to the spirit of the rococo. But an English restraint on the part of the artist does not allow the intrusion of any element which could impair the composure and deportment of William Wallis Lethieullier consistent with his "good breeding."[1]

William Wallis Lethieullier was a brother-in-law of Sir Matthew Fetherstonhaugh of Uppark, who commissioned this painting with eleven others in the years following his succession in 1740 to vast estates worth £400,000. William himself, the son of Christopher Lethieullier, a wealthy director of the Bank of England, had the means to enjoy the cultivated life of a gentleman of leisure with apparently no interest in the politics of his time.

The Fetherstonhaugh and Lethieullier families of the mid-eighteenth century are remembered as discriminating collectors and as members of learned societies, and it is in the latter context that they may have first made contact with other patrons of Devis.[2]

1. Compare with an engraving by Gravelot after Francis Hayman in the first illustrated edition of Samuel Richardson's *Pamela* (London, 1742, 6th edit., vol.1, opp. p.214) in which figures and subject are more closely related to each other.

2. As early as 1729, Smart Lethieullier (1701–1760), a near relation of William Wallis Lethieullier, was on friendly terms with John Byrom (Cat. 9) who apparently had interested him in his new system of shorthand. In later years both men were fellows of the Royal Society. For an association of the Lethieullier family with other Devis patrons see Cat. 35, 36.

PROVENANCE: By descent to the present owner.

REFERENCES: Pavière (12); D'Oench, list 102.

27. Mr. and Mrs. Van Harthals with their Son   1749   *P*

Signed and dated
Canvas, 34¾ × 46⅞ in.
The National Trust, Bearsted Collection, Upton House, Warwickshire

Little is known of Mr. Van Harthals, shown here with his wife and son. Apparently he was a Dutch merchant who lived at Gravesend. It is possible that Devis added a distant prospect of a winding river leading to the sea as an allusion to the Thames Estuary in that neighbourhood. On the other hand, the lack of positive identification of any topographical feature in the picture, and the presence of a telescope which points out to sea, held by Mrs. Van Harthals, makes it much more likely to represent the merchant's trading interests abroad.

The picture is remarkable for the extraordinary mannered pose of Mr. Van Harthals, who is represented here leaning against a tree trunk at almost forty-five degrees to the vertical. Perhaps the angular and wooden stance owes something to a too literal rendering of an awkwardly-articulating lay-figure.[1]

1. Such a lack of flexibility must have been common in artists' lay-figures. See letter written by John Wragg, an artists' colourman, Oct. 21, 1793, concerning the figure formerly owned by L. F. Roubiliac (Cat. 55).

PROVENANCE: Miss Montagu of Lowick Hall, Ulverston; her sale Christie's, June 29, 1928 (55), bt. by Martin for Lord Bearsted.

EXHIBITED: 25 Park Lane, London, *English Conversation Pieces,* 1930 (96), repr. pl.22; R.A., Winter, *British Art,* 1934 (336) *(Commemorative Catalogue,* 85); Arts Council, *English Conversation Pieces of the Eighteenth Century,* 1946 (13); British Council (Hamburg, Oslo, Stockholm, Copenhagen), *British Painting from Hogarth to Turner,* 1949 (37); Arts Council, touring exhibition, *Portrait Groups from National Trust Collections,* 1960 (21).

REFERENCES: Pavière (137); D'Oench, list 160; W. T. Whitley, 'Conversation Pieces of the 18th Century,' *The Collector,* IX, 1930, p.113, repr. 115; G. C. Williamson, *English Conversation Pieces.* London, 1931, pl.XII; S. H. Pavière, 'Arthur and Anthony Devis,' *Antique Collector,* V, 1934, p.4, repr.; S. H. Pavière, 'Biographical Notes on the Devis Family,' *Walpole Society,* XXV, 1937, p.122, No. 9.

28. Family Group in a Garden   1749

Signed and dated
Canvas, 40 × 49 in.
Private Collection, on loan to the Bowes Museum, Barnard Castle

It is unfortunate that in this, one of Devis' finest paintings, the identity of the sitters cannot be determined. It is thought to have been owned by the Cave-Brown-Cave family, and thence by descent to Geoffrey Clapham. There is, however, an interesting association with Sir Genille Cave-Brown-Cave, 12th Bt. (whose sister married William Wentworth Clapham in 1885), with Barlaston Hall, Staffordshire, once the home of the Wedgwood family. There is more than a coincidental similarity between this picture and the well-known Wedgwood family group painted by George Stubbs about 1780.[1] It would therefore seem likely that Stubbs may have seen it in the possession of the Wedgwoods or a close relative.

The painting is a masterpiece of compositional skill. Devis has set his stage on a terrace overlooking a regular river landscape. To the left three children playing with a small carriage adopt all the polite graces of the world of adults. Equidistant from the central axis of the picture, their parents pose with two other children and an elderly gentleman who is probably the father of the seated woman.

With its restrained use of colours, applied with the delicacy of a miniature painting, this picture is a perfect embodiment of English taste in the age of the rococo.

1. Wedgwood Museum, Barlaston, Staffordshire.

PROVENANCE: The Cave-Brown-Cave family; Sotheby's, Dick Collection Sale, April 1975; bt. present owner.

REFERENCES: D'Oench, list 249.

29. Sir George and Lady Strickland, of Boynton Hall, Bridlington, Yorkshire   1751

Signed indistinctly
Canvas, 35½ × 44½ in.
City of Kingston-upon-Hull Museums and Art Galleries, Ferens Art Gallery.

This proto-romantic landscape with Sir George and Lady Strickland is perhaps the nearest Arthur Devis ever approached to an English version of Arcadia. Sir George leans against a tree stump, while Elizabeth, Lady Strickland, sits on a fallen tree trunk and presents him with a piece of honeysuckle,

a symbol of endearment. Both figures, elegant in their deportment and in their gestures, perfectly reflect the refined reserve of the society which patronised Devis. The landscape background bears no recognisable relationship to the Boynton estate, and it is reasonable to assume that the artist transported his sitters into an imaginary landscape of his own choice.

An account book of the Strickland family[1] dates the picture in 1751, the year of the couple's marriage, which suggests that Devis was given the commission at the time of the sitters' return from their honeymoon.

The Stricklands were the descendants of a medieval family from Westmorland. Although they had been settled in Yorkshire since the sixteenth century, it is significant that they were related to the Stricklands of Nateby Hall, Garstang, Lancashire, who may well have recommended Devis to them for their portrait.[2]

Though his father, Sir William Strickland, was a chief spokesman of the government of the Whigs,[3] Sir George had little or no interest in politics. He was a member of the Society of Arts, and during his tenure of the Boynton estate he is said to have carried out many improvements there.

1. Arthur Oswald, Boynton Hall, Yorkshire — Formerly the Home of the Stricklands, *CL* 116, July 22, 1954, pp.282–83. D'Oench, Cat. 26.

2. See introduction with reference to the Devis family origins in Lancashire.

3. Romney Sedgwick, *The History of Parliament, The House of Commons, 1715–54* (H.M.S.O. London, 1970), vol.2, p.453.

PROVENANCE: By descent to Mrs. Anne Louise Strickland of Jersey; Sotheby's, June 18, 1969 (116), bt. Spink; bt. by the Ferens Art Gallery, December 1971 with the aid of a grant from the N.A.C.F. and other funds.

EXHIBITED: Leeds City Art Gallery, *Treasures from Yorkshire Houses*, 1947 (13); Bordeaux, Galerie des Beaux-Arts, *La Peinture Britannique de Gainsborough a Bacon*, 1977 (5); Yale Center for British Art, *The Conversation Piece: Arthur Devis and His Contemporaries*, New Haven, 1980 (26) repr.

REFERENCES: Pavière (128), repr. pl.28; Arthur Oswald, Boynton Hall, Yorkshire, — Formerly the Home of the Stricklands, *Country Life* 116, July 22, 1954, pp.282–283; J. D. Hunt and P. Willis, *The Genius of the Place, The English Landscape Garden, 1620–1820*, London, 1975, repr. pl.86; John Hayes, *Gainsborough*, London, 1975, repr. pl.22;

John Sunderland, *Painting in Britain, 1525–1975*, Oxford, 1976, repr. pl.50 and 51; D'Oench, Cat. 26, repr. with full bibliography.

30. The Swaine Family of Fencroft, Isle of Ely, Cambridgeshire   1749

Signed and dated
Canvas, 25¼ × 40¾ in.
Yale Center for British Art, Paul Mellon Collection, New Haven, Connecticut, U.S.A.

Little is known of the early provenance of this painting, and even its association with the Swaine family is only recorded for the first time this century.[1] In 1847 it was owned by John Lavicount Anderdon (1792–1874), an enthusiastic fisherman who published *The River Dove: with some private thoughts on the happy Practice of Angling*, 1847. It is reasonable to assume that he acquired it because its content reflected his sporting interest.

Ellen D'Oench[2] has identified the sitters as John Swaine, his wife, Alice, née Crosse, whom he married in 1744, their two children, Spelman (1745–1803) and Elizabeth, later to become the wife of Capt. Hepburn, and the gentleman on the right who is John Swaine the elder (c. 1681–1753), a London linen draper.

This English *fête-champêtre*[3] has a subject of unusual directness for Devis. So predominant is the angling theme, with the young boy and his grandfather holding fishing rods, fish and a net on the bank, and John Swaine himself apparently quoting from a book on the subject, that it must have been at the request of his patron.

1. In the collection of Arthur N. Gilbey of Sulhampstead, Berkshire, who purchased the painting c. 1908, as *The Swaine Family*. Until the exhibition *The Conversation Piece: Arthur Devis and His Contemporaries*, Yale Center for British Art, New Haven, 1980, with its catalogue by Ellen G. D'Oench, all references were to the Swaine family of Leverington (or Laverington) Hall, Isle of Ely, Cambridgeshire. That was, however, the seat of Daniel Swaine, brother of John Swaine the younger.

2. For further information see D'Oench (21), and also Judy Egerton, catalogue of the exhibition *British Sporting and Animal Paintings in the Mellon Collection, 1655–1867*, London, 1980 (59), in which the painting is described as *Family Group Beside a River (called The Swaine Family)*.

3. Devis' treatment of the subject is reminiscent of an engraving in a section 'Pleasure and Recreation' in George Bickham's *Universal Penman; or the Art of Writing Made Useful*, London, 1741, pl.85, dated December 1736, in which three children are shown in a rustic setting with a garden fork, a bucket, and a hat placed as a still life in the foreground.

PROVENANCE: John Lavicount Anderdon, 1847; H. Natalli, Isle of Ely, from whom it was bought by Arthur N. Gilbey, Sulhampstead, Berkshire; Christie's, April 25, 1940 (88); bt. Frost and Reed; J. C. Meyers, U.S.A.; Newhouse Galleries, 1969; Mr. and Mrs. Jack R. Dick, Greenwich, Conn.; Sotheby's, October 31, 1973 (7) bt. Roy Miles, from whom acquired by Paul Mellon.

EXHIBITED: Wembley, 1925 (V 30), repr. in illustr. souvenir, p.15; London, *English Conversation Pieces*, 1930 (105); R. A. *British Art*, 1934 (390), and in *Commemorative Catalogue of the Exhibition of British Art, 1934*, 1935 (86), repr. pl.XXIII; Preston, *Lancashire Art*, 1934 (35); London, *British Sporting and Animal Paintings in the Paul Mellon Collection, 1655–1867*, 1980 (59), repr. pl.10.

REFERENCES: Pavière (129); D'Oench, Cat. 21; Waltèr Shaw Sparrow, *Angling in British Art*, London, 1923, repr. opp. p.184; *Connoisseur* 72 (June 1925); G. C. Williamson, *English Conversation Pieces*, p.12, repr. pl.XXX; *Country Life* 75 (Jan. 13, 1934), repr. p.33; *Connoisseur* 93 (Feb. 1934), repr. p.83; *The Times* (March 19, 1940), repr. p.12; 'The Arthur Gilbey Angling Collection', *Connoisseur* (April 1940), repr. p.181; *Art News* 38 (April 25, 1940); W. Leon Soldes, *Masterpieces of British Art*, London, 1940, repr. pl.27 as by Arthur William Devis; Arthur Oswald, 'The Swaines of Leverington,' *Country Life* 103 (Feb. 13, 1948); Frederick Antal, *Hogarth and his Place in European Art*, London, 1962, p.240, n.50, pl.30A; Frank Davis, 'Resurrected Reputations,' *Country Life* 154 (December 20, 1973), repr. pl.1; *Connoisseur* 185 (January 1974): 85, repr. p.86, Fig. 8; *Apollo* 99 (January 1974), repr. p.76.

31. The Boldero Brothers, of Cornborough, Yorkshire   1752

Signed and dated
Canvas, 39¾ × 49⅞ in.
Yale University Art Gallery, Bequest of Helen Huntington Hull

Described by Pavière as *The Boldero Family in Stapleton Park, Yorkshire*, this painting has now been identified as *The Boldero Brothers, of Cornborough, Yorkshire*.[1] The identities of the sitters are said to be, from left to right, Lewyns Boldero (1708–83), John (1711–89) of Stapleton Park, Yorkshire, Edward Gale (died 1772), and Henry (1723–89), of Aviary Hill, Kent.

This painting is a fine example of a group of canvases of the 1750s, characterised by an extraordinary elongation of the figures. In particular the proportions of Lewyns Boldero give him a head less than one ninth the length of his body. The painting may be compared with the portrait of *Sir Robert Rich,* c. 1755–57, which has a similarly-proportioned figure and a closely related landscape background.

1. See D'Oench, Cat. 27.

PROVENANCE: By descent to Sir W. Barttelot, Bt., of Stopham House, Pullborough, Sussex; Christie's, June 19, 1911(145) as *Four Gentlemen in a Landscape with a Dog,* by Arthur William Devis, and dated 1763; bt. Agnew; Mr. and Mrs. F. S. Boldero, 1911; Agnew 1930, as *A Shooting Party;* Vincent Astor, New York, 1930; bequeathed by his wife, Helen Huntington Hull, to Yale University Art Gallery, 1977.

EXHIBITED: The above exhibition in Note 1.

REFERENCES: Pavière (11); D'Oench, Cat. 27, list 12; Valentine Lawford, Historic Houses: The Locusts, Dutchess County Home of Mrs. Lytle Hull, *Architectural Digest* 36, March 1979, repr. p.62.

32. Gentleman at a Sundial   c. 1755

Signed, but no date visible   *P*
Canvas, 29 × 24 in.
Private Collection

Devis painted several similar whole-length portraits throughout his career, the first of these being of *John Warde of Squerrye's Court, Kent,* dated 1749.[1]

In the elongation of the figure and the angularity of pose it can be compared with *The Boldero Brothers, of Cornborough, Yorkshire* (Cat. 31) and *John Lockwood of Dews Hall, Essex* (Cat. 35).

The unknown gentleman wearing a fashionable sporting coat with a low stand collar and lapels, with matching waistcoat and breeches, leans against a sundial, the design of which Devis probably obtained from an architects' pattern book.[2]

1. See D'Oench, list 166; reproduced in *Country Life,* 143, June 27, 1968.

2. Such pattern books were numerous. See Batty Langley, *The City and Country Builder's and Workmen's Treasury of Designs,* London, 1745, pl.CLI, for a page of such designs. From the detailed measurements given Devis could easily have constructed the sundial in perspective.

PROVENANCE: Unknown; bt. by the present owner.

33. Self-Portrait   c. 1754   *P*

Canvas, 30¼ × 25 in.
Harris Museum and Art Gallery, Preston

This portrait, formerly catalogued as *Self Portrait of Arthur William Devis,* Arthur's son, was identified as a self-portrait of Arthur himself by Ellen D'Oench.[1] It demonstrates a new direction in Devis' art, characterised by a strong chiaroscuro in the lighting of his figures, a method later to be adopted by Joseph Wright of Derby in such well-known works as *A Philosopher giving a Lecture on the Orrery* (c. 1763–65), and *An Experiment on a Bird in the Air Pump* (1768).

It is inscribed on the reverse *Portrait of the Artist Arthur Devis/by Arthur Devis.*

1. See D'Oench, list 50.

PROVENANCE: Probably by descent to Mrs. C. Tupper; anonymous sale, Christie's, Dec. 21, 1928 (13), bt. E. Parsons & Sons; sold to the Brook Street Galleries, London, 1938; Mr. Ichenhauser; purchased by Harris Museum and Art Gallery, 1938.

EXHIBITED: Preston, *Lancashire Art,* 1938 (1).

REFERENCES: Pavière, p.125, (46) as by Arthur William Devis; D'Oench, list 50.

34. Assheton Curzon, later Viscount Curzon, of Penn House, Buckinghamshire, with his Tutor, Dr. Mather   c. 1754

Canvas, 27¼ × 22 in.
Private Collection

Here we see Devis' newly-discovered romantic phase applied to a conversation piece. By exploiting the principle of a spotlight concentrating the drama on a stage, he emphasises the communication between Assheton Curzon and his tutor.

So powerful is the narrative element that one overlooks the strangeness of brightly-lit figures in a room so dark that details of the interior are hardly visible. Even more curious is the shadow on the floor which surely could only have been formed by a light source beyond the ceiling and behind the walls. The evidence of this picture suggests that Devis placed his lay-figures in a simple stage-set comprising the walls of a room, without a ceiling. This may also account for small decorative details in his interiors appearing to be drawn rather than modelled on the walls.

Assheton Curzon (1730–1820) was the second surviving son of Sir Nathaniel Curzon, 4th Bt., and Mary, daughter of Sir Ralph Assheton, 2nd Bt., M.P., of Middleton, Lancashire. He was educated at Westminster School, 1740–46, and Brasenose College, Oxford, 1747. He also employed Dr. Roger Mather (1719–68), who appears with him in this picture, to teach him the art of public speaking following his return as member of Parliament for Clitheroe in 1754.

In politics he was described as "A man of Tory principles, votes with the ministry, but sometimes affects to be conscientious by quitting the House when the minister's question is not agreeable to him."[1]

1. *Public Ledger*, 1779. See Sir Lewis Namier and John Brooke, *History of Parliament, The House of Commons, 1754–90* (H.M.S.O. 1964), vol.1, p.287.

PROVENANCE: By descent to Mary Cecil, 17th Baroness Zouch, and then to her daughter; Sotheby's, June 26, 1981; acquired by the present owner.

EXHIBITED: Yale Center for British Art, *The Conversation Piece: Arthur Devis and His Contemporaries*, New Haven, 1980(30), repr.

REFERENCES: Catalogue of the above exhibition.

35. John Lockwood of Dews Hall, Essex c. 1757   *P*

Canvas, 30 × 25 in.
Simon Cotton, Hertfordshire

This portrait, with its strong contrast of light and shade, and mannerist elongation of the figure, may be dated to a period shortly after the mid 1750s. It can be related to a portrait of Sir John Shaw, of Eltham Lodge, Kent,[1] in which all the essential features of the composition are repeated. It represents an extension of Devis' newly-discovered romantic phase, in which the sitter and his surroundings are psychologically more closely related to each other.

John Lockwood gazes introspectively towards the spectator; his features, caught in a strong chiaroscuro, blend into the autumnal foliage of the trees behind him. Devis has painted him as a sensitive and cultured man with a poetic rather than a materialistic frame of mind. Through his wife, Matilda Conyers, he was related to the Lethieullier (Cat. 26) and Fetherstonhaugh families, and also to Sir Roger Newdigate (Cat. 38) who married his sister-in-law, all of whom pursued antiquarian interests.

His brother-in-law, John Conyers, of Copt Hall, Essex, was a Tory member of Parliament for Reading (1747–54) and Essex (1772–75), and was the only male member of this closely-knit family circle not known to have been painted by Devis. However, there is a painting of the same date which shows an unknown gentleman sitting in an interior with two unframed portraits[2] propped up against the wall, one behind the other. The two women in the portraits may be John Conyer's wives, the first of whom, Hannah Warner, died in 1745.[3]

1. D'Oench, list 141.

2. For a photograph of this painting see Fig. 17 in the catalogue of the exhibition, *The Conversation Piece: Arthur Devis and His Contemporaries*, Yale Center for British Art, New Haven, 1980.

3. I am indebted to Simon Cotton, who owns the two Lockwood portraits (Cat. 35, 36), for this ingenious and plausible explanation for the existence of this enigmatic portrait.

PROVENANCE: By descent to the present owner.

EXHIBITED: Preston, *Lancashire Art*, 1937(26).

REFERENCES: Pavière (102); D'Oench, list 106.

36. Mrs. John Lockwood (née Matilda Conyers) of Dews Hall, Essex   c. 1757

Canvas, 30 × 25 in.   *P*
Simon Cotton, Hertfordshire

This portrait is a pendant to that of John Lockwood (Cat. 35). Mrs. Lockwood, formerly Matilda Conyers, of Copt Hall, Essex, sits playing a guitar in pensive melancholy before the entrance to a cave in the wilderness. Perhaps the most immediate source of its inspiration lay in the artificial grottos and rocky caves of the landscape gardeners' art, popularised by developments in English taste for the works of the 17th century Italian landscape painter, Salvator Rosa. It is also significant that numerous engravings after that artist were being published at the time. In particular Devis must have known an engraving *Landscape with a Cave* after Salvator Rosa, in which the cave and other features are similar to those in this painting.[1] The guitar is of the cittern shape, common in England throughout the eighteenth century.

No doubt because of its unusual subject it is singled out as an example of the artist's work in a brief biography written in Edward Edwards' *Anecdotes of Painters who have resided or been born in England*, published in London, 1808.

1. For a reproduction of this engraving see E. W. Manwaring, *Italian Landscape in Eighteenth Century England,* 2nd impression of the 1925 edition, Frank Cass and Co. Ltd., London, 1965.

PROVENANCE: By descent to the present owner.

EXHIBITED: Preston, *Lancashire Art,* 1937 (30).

REFERENCES: Pavière (101); *Walpole Society,* vol.25, 1936–37, repr. pl.xliii(a); *Antique Collector,* vol.8, April 1937, p.86; D'Oench, list 107.

ENGRAVING: See Edward Edwards, *Anecdotes of Painters who have resided or been born in England,* London, 1808, p.123, as *Miss Conyers, of Copthall, Essex,* engraved by Thomas Chambers.

37. John, second Lord Monson, with his eldest Son, John, in Broxbournebury Park, Hertfordshire   c.1756   P

Canvas, 25 × 29½ in.
Mrs. William Dalison Keown-Boyd, on loan to the Harris Museum and Art Gallery, Preston

John, second Lord Monson, was the eldest son of John, Baron Monson of Burton, in the County of Lincoln, and Margaret Watson, third and youngest daughter of Lewis, Earl of Rockingham. He was born in 1727, and married Theodosia, daughter of John Maddison of Harpswell, Lincolnshire, in 1752.

His brother George, acting on his behalf, was elected as member of Parliament for Lincoln in 1754, in what even for those times was a corrupt and expensive campaign. Referring to this event in a letter to Sir John Ligonier in November 1757, the Duke of Newcastle wrote of how "his brother my Lord Monson spent above £6000 to choose him for Lincoln."[1] The Monson family were generally supporters of the Whigs, but it is significant that Lord Monson's brother did not vote with the Government on the land tax bill on February 27, 1767.

Lord Monson is shown here with his son, John, in the undulating landscape garden of Broxbournebury Park, a mansion which the family had owned since 1645. A model of politeness, he sits relaxed without affectation, his feet slightly apart and turned out at an angle of forty-five degrees. A curious feature is the way in which father and son stare intently beyond the confines of the picture frame, indicating the presence of someone to the left of the spectator. This tension between things seen and unseen lends a dramatic dimension to the content of the picture which relates it to narrative painting.

The apparent friendship between the Monson family and the Duke of Newcastle, uncle of Henry Fiennes Clinton, ninth Earl of Lincoln, may have gained Devis the commission for this portrait (See Cat. 40).

1. For further information on George Monson see Sir Lewis Namier and John Brooke, *The History of Parliament, The House of Commons, 1754–90,* (H.M.S.O. 1964), vol.3, pp.151–52.

PROVENANCE: By descent to the present owner.

38. Sir Roger Newdigate in his library at Arbury Hall, Warwickshire   c.1756–58

Canvas, 35 × 30 in.
Trustees of the Newdigate Settlement

The date of this painting and the time Devis required for its completion may be determined from Sir Roger Newdigate's entry in his diary for May 3, 1756, when he sat for his picture "at Davies's," and for May 10, 1758, two years later, when he sat again to "finish it."

Sir Roger Newdigate (1719–1806), fifth baronet of Harefield, Middlesex, and Arbury, Warwickshire, was descended from an ancient family which traced its ancestry back to the reign of King John. He was the seventh son of Sir Richard Newdigate, and Elizabeth, daughter of Sir Roger Twisden.

Newdigate was an assiduous member of Parliament, and his notebooks of the day's proceedings in the House are a valuable source of information on parliamentary debates in the eighteenth century. His political career began when he was returned for Middlesex in 1742, a seat which he held until 1747. He represented Oxford University from 1751 to 1780, having been proposed by his close friend and supporter, James Clitherow of Boston House, Brentford, Middlesex.[1] He was a high Tory whose principles transcended mere party matters, and a rigid adherent of the Church of England, opposed to any change in its liturgy, constitution, or privileges. He is often regarded as having been a Jacobite. However, he was politically independent and refused to join any county association for raising troops to assist the Young Pretender. This reluctance which may well have been dictated by political prudence, may be responsible for Horace Walpole's well-known description of him as a "half-converted Jacobite."

Newdigate is also remembered as an antiquarian and a collector of ancient marbles. From 1738 to 1740 he made the Grand Tour to France, Italy and the Netherlands, and later in life, following the death of his wife in 1774, he once more visited the continent, where he amassed a vast collection of paintings and sculptures to adorn his magnificent mansion, Arbury Hall, which he had rebuilt in the 'gothick' style.

Here he is shown seated at his Chippendale desk in his library.[2] Beyond is a portrait of his wife, painted by William Hoare.

Devis may have gained his commission through the recommendation of other patrons to whom Sir Roger Newdigate was related by marriage. His first wife, Sophia, was a sister of Matilda Conyers (Cat. 36), and a great-grand-daughter of Anne Lethieullier.[3] His second wife, Hester, was the daughter of Edward Mundy of Shipley, Derbyshire.

An interesting feature in the painting is the distortion of perspective which lends a surrealist quality to the placing of the figure and the desk in the room, and also gives the impression that the floor is tilting towards the spectator. This is common in works by other artists at the time, and may have been due to misleading illustrations in some text books on perspective available to them.

1. Devis painted James Clitherow and his wife, Anne, in the grounds of their manor house at Brentford, Middlesex, in 1759. For further information see D'Oench, Cat. 37.

2. See D'Oench, p.23; Michael McCarthy, "Sir Roger Newdigate: Drawings for Copt Hall, Essex, and Arbury Hall, Warwickshire," *Architectural History*, 16 (1973), repr. p.29; see also John Cornforth, "Painters and Georgian Interiors," *Country Life*, 161, Jan. 27, 1977.

3. For reference to the Lethieullier family see Cat. 26.

PROVENANCE: By descent to the present owner.

EXHIBITED: Birmingham, *Art Treasures in the Midlands*, 1934(243); Birmingham, *Works of Art from Midland Houses*, 1953(15); R. A., *Eighteenth Century Taste*, 1955–56 (305).

REFERENCES: Pavière (110); D'Oench, list 120, and p.23; H. M. Colvin, *Dictionary of English Architects*, 1954, pp.281, 336; and as above in note 2.

39. Sir Robert Rich, of Ross Hall, Suffolk, and Waverley Abbey, Surrey   1756–58

Signed   P
Canvas, 23¾ × 16⅝ in.
The Trustees of the Museum of the King's Own Royal Regiment, City Museum, Lancaster

Sir Robert Rich (1714–85) was the eldest surviving son of field-marshall Sir Robert Rich, the Whig politician. He followed his father into a military career, but unlike him had comparatively little interest in politics. He is principally remembered for his heroic rôle in the battle of Culloden on April 16, 1746, when his left hand was chopped off and his right arm almost severed above the elbow.[1] He is said to have been carried from the battlefield by his chaplain, John Duncan, to whom he bequeathed this portrait as a token of remembrance.

He was elevated to the rank of lieutenant-general in 1760, having been appointed governor of Londonderry only two years before.[2] However, in later years he was involved in a scandal over alleged deficiencies in the equipment of the soldiers of the 4th Dragoons, of which regiment his father had been colonel. This ultimately led to his dismissal from the governorship, and from the service in 1774.

Here he is shown wearing a black coat, a gold-embroidered waistcoat, and red breeches. Not only has Devis made no attempt to disguise the loss of his patron's left hand, but has highlighted it by placing the open coat sleeve in juxtaposition with the scars of a lopped-off branch on an oak tree against which Sir Robert is leaning.

Two versions of the portrait exist,[3] and this may be accounted for by the artist being required to paint portraits for the estates of both Ross Hall and Waverley Abbey.

The painting is set in a splendid eighteenth-century frame embellished with trophies of war.

1. See L. E. Cowper, *The King's Own*, vol.1; *Letters of Horace Walpole*, Ed. Peter Cunningham, London, 1891, vol.II, p.19, letter dated April 25, 1746.

2. April 24, 1756.

3. See photograph, Witt Library, of version signed and dated 1758.

PROVENANCE: Bequeathed to his chaplain, John Duncan, 1785; given by his descendant, Miss Duncan, to Sir Charles Rich, 4th Bt.; given by Lady Rich to the King's Own Regimental Museum, August, 1937.

40. Henry Fiennes Clinton, ninth Earl of Lincoln, with his Wife, Catherine, and Son, George   c. 1751

Canvas, 47½ × 66½ in.
Private Collection

Henry Fiennes Clinton was the second son of Henry Clinton, seventh Earl of Lincoln, and Lucy Pelham, sister of the Rt. Hon. Henry Pelham, the Prime Minister. He succeeded his brother, George, as ninth Earl on April 30, 1730. His relationship to the Pelham family, particularly after his marriage in 1744 to Catherine Pelham, daughter of the Prime Minister, enabled him to gain great influence in politics, where he was eagerly cultivated by the Whig party.

From being elected Lord Lieutenant of Cambridgeshire in 1742, he further advanced himself by obtaining the financially-rewarding sinecure of Comptroller of the Customs in the Port of London. In 1751, about the time this picture was painted, he received the Order of the Garter from George II.

However, he had little or no interest in politics, and is perhaps more remembered for his amorous pursuits which were celebrated in a questionable ode written by Sir Charles Hanbury Williams. This may well account for the reaction of Lady Carteret to his impending marriage, as recalled in a letter written by Horace Walpole to Sir Horace Mann on July 22, 1744. On being told "that Lord Lincoln had promised to make a very good husband to Miss Pelham, Lady Carteret, with an accent of energy, replied, "J'espère qu'il tiendra sa promesse!""[1]

The young boy in the painting is George, Lord Clinton, born October 26, 1745, in Downing Street, Westminster. His godfathers were King George II, and Thomas Holles, Duke of Newcastle, and his godmother the Duchess of Rutland. He died August 19, 1752 at Greenwich House.

The painting is interesting in that it is probably the one referred to in an uncomplimentary letter written by Lord John Cavendish in 1765, to Lady Dorothy Cavendish, his niece. In describing how Devis had unfortunately been selected to paint a portrait of William, 5th Duke of Devonshire, he suggests that *"I am much afraid it will be frightful for I understand, his pictures are all of a sort; they are whole lengths of about two feet long; and the person is always represented in a genteel attitude, either leaning against a pillar, or standing by a flower pot, or leading an Italian greyhound in a string, or in some other such ingenious posture. Your brother says He will submit quickly to whatever the Painter pleases, but will take great care not to give any opinion of his own, that He may not be answerable to any of its absurditys."*[2] The painting,

reproduced in colour in this catalogue, is a fine example of the work of the artist. Lord John Cavendish is not entirely accurate in his description of the attitudes taken up by the figures in Devis' pictures, in spite of the fact that he suggests he is familiar with his work.

1. *Letters of Horace Walpole,* Ed. P. Cunningham, vol.I, pp.315–17.

2. MSS P w G 101, University of Nottingham. See also D'Oench, p.31, and Ellis Waterhouse, *Painting in Britain, 1530–1790,* 4th ed. 1978, p.194.

PROVENANCE: The Earl of Lincoln; Christie's, March 31, 1939(14); bt. Agnew; repr. in sale catalogue; Frank Partridge; Mrs. Basil and the Hon. Mrs. Ionides, Buxted Park; purchased by present owner 1964.

REFERENCES: Pavière (165); D'Oench, list 34, and p.31.

41. Edward Gordon, his Sister Mrs. Miles, and her Husband in their Garden at Bromley, Kent   1756

Signed and dated
Canvas, 28½ × 40½ in.
Leicestershire Museums and Art Galleries, Leicester

In the painting of the Earl of Lincoln, his wife, and child (Cat. 40), we have already seen a new spatial awareness in the placing of figures in an open landscape. In this work, and in the following one (Cat. 42), Devis develops the idea still further. Hitherto he had depicted the landscape in naturalistic terms, or as it had been improved in the hands of the landscape gardeners,[1] but here in these two major canvases of the mid 1750s he introduces a classical element which demonstrates the influence on him of the paintings of Claude Lorrain.[2]

Set against this English version of a classical landscape, the artist places Mr. and Mrs. Miles on a balustraded terrace before their house at Bromley, Kent. The coat which Mr. Miles is wearing has long cuffs, which were very popular with men of fashion during the mid 1750s. He has removed his three-cornered hat, placing it behind him on the balustrade, and reveals that he has a wig with a toupée. Mrs. Miles, just as fashion-conscious, wears a sack with a wide stomacher and narrow robings, sleeve flounces and ruffles. Another feature of her costume which was popular at the time is a petticoat trimmed with a flounce and furbelows. To the right, Edward Gordon, wearing his three-cornered hat placed sensibly on his head,[3] presents

59

a pheasant to the couple. In this painting the figures adopt a naturalness in their deportment which avoids the excessive artificial formality regarded in polite circles as a contradiction of good breeding.

Also worthy of mention is the carefully constructed perspective of the terrace, which splendidly integrates into the landscape beyond. Two years before this picture was painted Devis had acquired a copy of *Dr. Brook Taylor's Method of Perspective Made Easy,*[4] an investment which had certainly proved to be worthwhile.

1. In a portrait dated 1743, Devis placed Robert Gwillym and William Farington in an Italianate landscape similar to those on the walls in many interiors in his paintings. See illustration, D'Oench, Cat. 9.

2. Towards the middle of the 18th century there was an increasing popularity in England for the works of the 17th century landscape painter, Claude Lorrain. This was reflected in engravings after paintings by him in English collections, notably by Vivares, Canot, Mason and Wood, between the years 1741 and 1746. Devis of course may have seen the actual paintings, but he would certainly have been familiar with the engravings.

3. In a letter written to his son, Dec. 30, O.S.1748, Lord Chesterfield suggested that "Any affectation whatsoever in dress, implies, in my mind, a flaw in the understanding. Most of our young fellows here (London) display some character or other by their dress; some effect the tremendous, and wear a great and fiercely-cocked hat, an enormous sword, a short waistcoat and a black cravat; these I should be almost tempted to swear the peace against, in my own defence, if I were not convinced that they are but meek asses in lions' skins."

4. Devis apparently subscribed to the volume in 1754. See chronology in the catalogue of the exhibition, *The Conversation Piece: Devis and His Contemporaries,* Yale Center for British Art, New Haven, 1980.

PROVENANCE: By descent through the Gordon family to Capt. H. Gordon, always as by Reynolds; C. F. G. Gordon; Sotheby's Dec. 10, 1925(90) as by Reynolds; Leggat Bros.; S. Arthur Peto; Mrs. J. L. Cross; presented by her to the present owners in 1955, as by Reynolds.

EXHIBITED: Grosvenor Gallery, 1884(207) as by Reynolds.

REFERENCES: Sir Walter Armstrong, *Sir Joshua Reynolds*, p.208; Grazes and Cronin, *History of the Works of Reynolds*, vol.1, p.373; D'Oench, list 67. Reviews of the Grosvenor Gallery exhibition in *The Queen*, Jan. 19, 1884, and *Pall Mall Gazette*, Jan. 3, 1884.

42. Edward Parker and his Wife, Barbara, née Fleming, on the Terrace at Browsholme Hall, near Clitheroe 1757 NPG

Signed and dated
Canvas, 50 × 40 in.
The Leger Galleries Ltd., London

This masterly example of Devis' middle phase is a triumph of sophisticated organisation. Painted with naive charm, Edward Parker and his wife Barbara stand on a terrace placed diagonally in the picture plane. Beyond them a tree, inspired by the landscapes of Claude, frames a majestic prospect comprising a river valley with waterfall, a church, and a mountain range, brought together in a complex spatial arrangement. To the right is a rustic stable from which has emerged a horse and groom, no doubt an allusion to the sporting interests of Edward Parker, who is shown here wearing spurs. It has been suggested that the landscape was inspired by the countryside around Dallam Tower, Westmorland, but the two principal features, the unusual church tower and stable occur in other quite unrelated paintings.[1] Edward Parker is shown wearing a fashionable frock-coat with large lapels and a matching waistcoat and breeches. In his hand he holds a cane, which in eighteenth-century England was considered a safer and more appropriate alternative to the carrying of a sword. In keeping with his sporting interests he wears his three-cornered hat sharply tilted backwards. In all probability Barbara Parker never owned the sumptuous blue sack and petticoat trimmed with flounce and furbelows. It appears in a variety of different colours in several paintings by Devis and was most probably a small costume used on a lay-figure in his London studio (see Cat. 55 and 56).

Edward Parker (1730–1794) was a passionate sympathiser with the Stuart cause in his youth. In this he had the support of his father's cousin, Thomas Lister, member of Parliament for Clitheroe, and "a strong and sour Jacobite."[2]

Edward Parker is shown in the painting with Barbara Fleming whom he had married in 1750. She was the daughter and co-heiress of Sir William Fleming of Rydall Hall, Westmorland.

1. See Cat. 45 for the same church. A portrait of a *'Gentleman and Lady by a Porch'* c. 1756–57, (phot. Cooper 740857), present location unknown, has the same barn seen from a different angle and the identical horse and groom before it.

2. Romney Sedgwick, *The History of Parliament, The House of Commons, 1715–54* (H.M.S.O. London 1970), vol.2, p.219.

PROVENANCE: Edward Parker; by descent to Daniel Wilson of Dallam Tower, Westmorland, nephew of his wife; by descent to Sir Maurice Bromley-Wilson, Bt; Christie's, March 13, 1970 (76); bt. Leger Galleries; private collection; Leger Galleries.

EXHIBITED: Preston, Harris Museum and Art Gallery, *Twelfth Annual Spring Exhibition of Work by Lancashire Artists, including a Special Loan Exhibition of Work by Members of the Devis Family,* 1937 (14); London, The Leger Galleries, *English Paintings 1750–1900,* Oct 1970 (2) repr; Yale Center for British Art, *The Conversation Piece: Arthur Devis and His Contemporaries,* New Haven, 1980, Cat. 34, repr. in colour.

REFERENCES: Pavière (115); Pavière, Arthur and Anthony Devis, *Antique Collector,* April 1934, p.42; Pavière, Biographical Notes on the Devis Family of Painters, *Walpole Society, 1936–7, vol. XXV,* repr; Pavière, The Devis Exhibition at Preston, *C. L.* March 13, 1937, repr. pl.ix; *Illustrated London News,* March 20, 1937, p.503; *The Sphere,* Preston holds a Devis Loan Exhibition, March 20, 1937, p.451; *Connoisseur,* October 1970, p.149; D'Oench, Cat. 34, repr. in colour.

43. Edward Parker, of Browsholme Hall, near Clitheroe   1757   *P*

Signed and dated
Canvas, 30 × 25 in.
Private Collection

This portrait shows Edward Parker striking an identical pose to that in the previous catalogue entry. Devis has, however, exchanged the costumes on his lay-figure for a bright red frock (a coat with a turned-down collar), a brilliant, contrasting blue waistcoat with gold trimmings, and yellow breeches.

The landscapes in both paintings are again closely related, with a stable to the right seen from exactly the same view-point; but the comparative flatness of the terrain and the substitution of a horse fence for the terrace in the foreground of this picture strongly suggests that the artist was not attempting a topographical description of any particular place.

A feature of this painting (and also of the portrait of Edward Parker and his wife, Barbara) is its fairly pronounced chiaroscuro which links it with Devis' short-lived experiments in the dramatic use of light and shade in the immediately preceding years.

Another portrait in the same collection, formerly thought to be of John Parker (1695–1754)[1]

is probably Robert Parker of Alkincoats, who married Elizabeth, Edward Parker's sister, and whose eldest son was born in 1753.[2]

1. See D'Oench, Cat. 34.

2. Pedigree of Parker of Browsholme, and Alkincoats, in Joseph Foster, *Pedigrees of the County Families of England,* vol.1, Lancashire, 1873.

PROVENANCE: By descent to the present owner.

EXHIBITED: Preston, *Lancashire Art,* 1934(33).

REFERENCES: Pavière (113); D'Oench, p.61, list 125.

44. Col. John Sabine, and his Family, in the Park at Tewin House, Hertfordshire c. 1758

Canvas, 37 × 50½ in.
Private Collection

The late 1750s mark a new but transient development in Devis' art which is well illustrated in this painting.[1] The artist has monumentalised his sitters by drawing them from a low position relative to the horizon, in an open space on a rising incline. This, together with the horizontal lines of the undulating lawn, introduces a classical element which contrasts with the angularity of the figures.

John Sabine (1712–76) was the son of General Sir Joseph Sabine (c. 1661–1739), Commander-in-Chief of the allied forces in Belgium and Holland under Marlborough. He was educated at Westminster School and Trinity College, Cambridge, and in 1742 married Susannah Osborne, by whom he had a son, Joseph, and a daughter, Dianna Amelia. He was commissioned in his father's regiment soon after his birth. In 1742 he was transferred to the 1st Foot Guards and fought in the war of the Austrian Succession.

An inscription[2] on the reverse identifies the sitters and also the landscape background with Tewin House and church. Tewin House, bought by John Sabine's father with money given to him by Queen Anne for his services to the nation, was said to be furnished so magnificently that George I is alleged to have visited it twice under the pretext of going hunting.[3] The house was demolished in 1807, but the church, just visible in the picture, still survives.

1. For other similar paintings see *The Cross Family, of Shudy Camps Park, Cambridgeshire,* (Phot. Witt) and *The Maynard Family in the Park at Waltons, Essex,* repr. D'Oench, Cat. 38.

61

2. The inscription reads *At our death with our love this Family Picture from Sir F. S. Pasley, and after his son Maitland Pasley, The persons are: John & Edward Sabine's father sitting on the ground, their Aunt afterwards Mrs. Petty sitting on a garden roller and on the right of the picture their grandfather and grandmother Mr. and Mrs. Sabine. In the background are the church and family house of Tewin. The house is pulled down, but the church continues and the Family Vault is there.* Another inscription reads *At my death, this picture is to go to my sister Loni for her life, and then to Montague Wynyard Sabine Pasley, Royal Artillery. Desmond son of my late brother Major Maitland B. W. Sabine Pasley, Royal Artillery. G. S. Pasley June 2nd 1899.*

3. Romney Sedgwick, *The History of Parliament, The House of Commons, 1715–54* (H.M.S.O. London 1970), vol.2, p.398.

PROVENANCE: By descent to G. S. Pasley, 1899; by descent to Major Maitland B. W. Sabine Pasley; Major General J. M. S. Pasley sale, Christie's, June 21, 1974 (141); acquired by the present owner.

REFERENCES: D'Oench, list 133.

45. Alicia and Jane Clarke, of Walford Court, Ross-on-Wye, Herefordshire c. 1758

Signed and dated
Canvas, 36 × 28 in.
Private Collection

This painting, with its extraordinary decorative richness, brings together all those aspects of the art of Devis which make his paintings memorable. Alicia and Jane Clarke, daughters of Richard Clarke, of Walford Court, Ross-on-Wye, pose in a wooded glade near Walford church. The figure to the left is wearing a blue costume identical to that worn by Mrs. Parker in Cat. 42. The other, seated against a tree stump, shows off to advantage her magnificent pink sack with sleeve flounces and ruffles, and matching petticoat.

It is possible that Devis obtained the commission for this painting through members of the Farington family, of Leyland, Lancashire, who lived in Herefordshire.[1]

1. Margaret and Isabella Farington, daughters of William Farington and Elizabeth Rufine of Hereford, and sisters of the Rev. William Farington (See Cat. 7), married respectively the Rev. John Woodcock of Canon Pion, Herefordshire, and William Bissell of Seaburnes, in the same county.

PROVENANCE: By descent; Sotheby's, July 6, 1977(12); bt. Agnew; Richard Thune, Connecticut; Private Collection.

EXHIBITED: London, Thos. Agnew & Sons, *Three Centuries of British Paintings*, 1978(2), repr. on cover; Yale Center for British Art, *The Conversation Piece: Arthur Devis and His Contemporaries*, New Haven, 1980(35), repr.

REFERENCES: The two catalogues of the above exhibitions.

46. Wills Hill, 1st Earl of Hillsborough, with his Family   c. 1753–54

Canvas, 25 × 30¼ in.
Trustees of the Marchioness of Downshire Discretionary Settlement, on loan to the National Portrait Gallery

The painting can be dated stylistically and by the absence of a third child, Charlotte, born in 1754. Compositionally, it is related to *Gentleman and Lady in a Landscape,* 1748 (Cat. 16), but by comparison it possesses a greater integration of its component parts. In terms of colour and aerial perspective the landscape background convincingly sets the figures in space, avoiding any suggestion that it is a painted backcloth on a stage.

Wills Hill (1718–1793), 1st Earl of Hillsborough, was the son of Trevor, Viscount Hillsborough, and Mary, daughter of Anthony Rowe of North Aston, Oxfordshire. He is shown here with his wife, Margaret, daughter of Robert, Earl of Kildare, and two of his children, Arthur, who succeeded him as the second Marquis, and Mary Amelia, who later married the Marquis of Salisbury and was burnt to death in a fire at Hatfield House in 1835.

Wills Hill is remembered for his leading rôle in the politics of his time. His career began in 1741 when he entered Parliament as an Opposition Whig as member for Warwick. About the year 1750 he transferred his allegiance to the Pelhams, which gained for him the high offices of Comptroller of the Household, 1754–55, and Treasurer of the Chamber, 1755–56, under the Newcastle Administration. In later years he was constituted Commissioner of Trade and Plantations, 1763, Joint Postmaster-General, 1766, and Secretary of State for the Colonies, 1768–72. He was re-appointed Secretary in 1779, and as one of the leaders of the administration had to shoulder much of the unpopularity of the American War. In his time he was regarded as a well-bred, handsome man with agreeable manners, but opinions wildly differed as to his political skills. While Horace Walpole regarded him as one of the foremost speakers in the House, George III is known to have said of him "Lord Hillsborough always put things off to the last minute, and though an amiable man (is) the least man of business I ever knew."[1]

The painting is inscribed *Wills Hill . Earl of Hillsborough/Margaretta: Countss of Hillsborough./ Viscount Kilwarlin & Lady Mary Amelia Hill.*

1. See Sir Lewis Namier and John Brooke, *The History of Parliament, the House of Commons, 1754–90* (H.M.S.O. 1964), vol.2, pp.626, 627.

PROVENANCE: By descent to the present owner.

EXHIBITED: Presently on loan to the National Portrait Gallery from the Trustees of the Marchioness of Downshire Discretionary Settlement.

REFERENCES: D'Oench, list 78.

47. Gentleman with a Horse   c. 1760–63

Canvas, 29½ × 24½ in.   *P*
Private Collection

This fine example of a single whole-length from Devis' late period contrasts with many of his earlier works in having a more carefully considered integration of the component parts of its composition. The subtle rhythms in the stance of the gentleman holding a whip in his right hand are complemented by the simple curvilinear forms of a river landscape in which all detail not essential to the subject has been excluded.

An unusual feature in the painting is the intrusion of the horse's head on the left, a device used by Devis to indicate the animal's presence without having to confront the problems of painting it in its entirety.[1]

The unknown gentleman in the picture wears a sporting coat with lapels and mariner's cuffs. As with the portraits of Edward Parker (Cat. 42, 43) the artist has given his three-cornered hat a sporting backward tilt.

1. See D'Oench, Cat. 4. *Thomas Lister and His Family at Gisburne Park, Clitheroe, Yorkshire* for further reference on this method used by Devis.

PROVENANCE: The Hon. F. Wallop; Spink and Son, 1976; bt. by the present owner.

EXHIBITED: Harris Museum and Art Gallery, 1950.

REFERENCES: Pavière (61); D'Oench, list 223.

48. Richard Lowe, Esq., of Denby and Locko Park, Derbyshire   c. 1761–62

Canvas, 30 × 24 in.
Captain P. J. B. Drury-Lowe, Locko Park, Derbyshire

Richard Lowe, of Denby and Locko Park, surveys his estates cast in an heroic mould which momentarily takes us away from the affectations of the polite society which patronised Devis. Here there is a grace and dignity,[1] a sense of spatial awareness, and a dramatic use of light and shade in a succession of receding horizontal planes, which shows a willingness to experiment with concepts formulated by a new generation of English artists.

Richard Lowe is wearing the costume of a fashionable country gentleman. Of particular interest is the round hat which was then becoming popular for sporting activities.

1. The natural stance adopted by the figure contrasts with the angularity of articulation so often to be found in Devis' portraits (Cat. 39), and may indicate that in this case he based his subject on a drawing from life rather than on a lay-figure.

PROVENANCE: By descent to the present owner.

EXHIBITED: Birmingham, *Works of Art from Midland Houses* (14), 1953; Nottingham. *Pictures from Locko Park* (32), 1968; Nottingham, *Masterpieces from Great Houses in the East Midlands* (12), 1981; Nottingham, *Locko Park and the Drury Lowes* (24).

REFERENCES: Reproduced in colour on the front of the *Connoisseur,* June 1976, which contained an article 'Locko Park, an important family collection,' by Richard Calvocoressi; D'Oench, list 108.

49. Elizabeth and Charlotte Edgar, of Red House Park, Ipswich, Suffolk   1762

Signed and dated   *P*
Canvas, 33⅜ × 39½ in.
The National Trust, Bearsted Collection, Upton House, Warwickshire

This charming and unusual picture of Elizabeth and Charlotte Edgar may be the one exhibited by Devis at the Free Society in 1763(55), where it was called *Two young ladies, with grapes, etc.; in a landscape.*[1] The two children are standing on the terrace of a mansion. Elizabeth, the elder sister, holds a basket and presents a bunch of grapes to Charlotte, who is holding a peach.

As is so often the case in Devis' paintings, the children stand out in sharp contrast to their surroundings. This curious feature, in which even the accompanying dogs merge tonally into the terrace pavement, lends a surrealist aspect to the painting.

Charlotte Edgar, born in 1757, married General François Hugonin, 4th Dragoons, of Nursted, near Petersfield, in whose family the picture remained until 1929.

1. It was not unusual for artists exhibiting at the Free Society to enter their works without the names of the sitters being included in the catalogue. Horace Walpole's annotated catalogues (See *Walpole Society*, vol.27, 1938–39 for a transcription) have been particularly valuable in identifying many unknown portraits in the exhibitions of the Society of Artists and the Free Society.

PROVENANCE: By descent; National Trust.

EXHIBITED: Free Society of Artists, 1763(55); London, *English Conversation Pieces*, 1930(103), repr.; London, Arts Council, *English Conversation Pieces*, 1946(16); Whitechapel Art Gallery, 1955(6).

REFERENCES: Pavière (36); D'Oench, list 57.

50. Francis Vincent, his Wife Mercy, and Daughter Ann, of Weddington Hall, Warwickshire   1763
Signed and dated
Canvas, 42 × 39⅝ in.
Harris Museum and Art Gallery, Preston

An extraordinary feature of this late example of the work of Devis is the vertical division of the composition into two separate halves, with only a tenuous rapport between father and child to link them together. The narrative content of the painting is now lost, but at the time the artist was commissioned to paint the picture, Francis Vincent of the Inner Temple, Barrister-at-Law, received a message worthy to be recorded in his family history.[1] Here he is shown presenting the letter to his wife, Mercy, who stares fixedly towards the spectator, leaving her daughter, Ann, uncomprehendingly presenting a sprig of honeysuckle to her father.

Mercy, a prisoner of fashion, is forced into a rigid upright posture by a stiffly-boxed bodice. The blue dress with lace sleeves and ruched trimmings which she is wearing must have been a lay-figure costume, since it appears in several paintings which Devis executed at the time. Similarly, Francis Vincent wears a red and green hussar's costume not unlike those on display in the exhibition (Cat. 56) and known to have been owned by the artist. As is so often the case in Devis' paintings, the landscape bears no relation to the parkland around the former Weddington Hall, and is to be found with slight variations in other works by the artist.[2]

Francis Vincent was the son of George Vincent of Colney Hatch, Middlesex, and Ann, daughter of Francis Stonard of the parish of St. Botolph, Bishopgate, London. Mercy, his wife, was the daughter of the Rev. Dormer Sheldon of Abberton, Worcestershire. She first married Thomas Adderley of Weddington Hall, who died in 1757. The following year she married Francis Vincent, who himself died on December 20, 1766, aged 40. The young child in the painting is Ann, born 1759–60. There is, however, a question as to why a son, Dormer Vincent, born c. 1761, is not included in the painting.

1. A note written at the time the picture was relined, c. 1900, records that the envelope on the ground bore the inscription "Sir Frederick Vincent, Weddington Hall, Warwickshire." This is not now visible. No Frederick Vincent ever lived at the hall, and it is probable that the abbreviation Fr. was expanded into the wrong christian name. The content of the letter is now lost.

2. See a similar landscape in the painting *Gentleman in a Landscape, possibly Lieut. John Grey*, 1758 (Phot. Cooper 333886).

PROVENANCE: T. B. Wirgman; Miss L. Thevenard, 1925, from whom purchased by the Harris Museum and Art Gallery, 1957.

REFERENCES: *The Times*, Sept. 11, 1957; D'Oench, list 165.

51. Edward Rookes-Leeds and His Family, of Royds Hall, Low Moor, Yorkshire c. 1763–68
Canvas, 36 × 49 in.
Private Collection

This is one of the last great conversation piece paintings of Devis' career, and is characterised by an attention to detail which extends from the splendid shimmering costumes in the foreground to the riverscape beyond.

Edward Rookes-Leeds takes up an elegant pose wearing matching coat, waistcoat, and breeches. A three-cornered hat is placed soberly on his head in marked contrast to those tilted backwards at a sporting angle in the portraits of *Edward Parker* (Cat. 42, 43) and *Gentleman with a Horse* (Cat. 47). He is looking towards his second wife, Henrietta, second from the left, daughter of Sandford Hardcastle, of Wakefield, and the three daughters of his previous marriage to Mary Leeds, of Milford. The daughters represented here are Mary (1742–1803) who married George Walker of Middleford Hall, Jane who married William Sergeantson of Wakefield, and Anne who married the Rev. Jeremiah Smith of Woodside, Sussex. The absence of another daughter, Elizabeth, who died in 1763, dates the picture some time between that year and 1768 when the daughter Jane died. Edward Rookes-Leeds was a spendthrift who became hopelessly involved in financial difficulties in 1781. He committed suicide in 1787 and his estates were sold to meet his liabilities.

The estate he owned near Bradford, said to be represented in this picture but more likely to have been invented by Devis, was rich in coal and iron. The Low Moor Iron Works was founded there and subsequently became the largest of its kind in the world.

PROVENANCE: By descent to a private collection in Yorkshire; acquired by Arthur Tooth and Sons, 1938; private collection; by descent to the present owners.

EXHIBITED: London, Arts Council, 1946(15), repr. pl.15; Royal Academy, *Exhibition of British Portraits,* 1956–57(339); Kenwood (14), repr. pl.V.B.; Yale Center for British Art, *The Conversation Piece: Arthur Devis and His Contemporaries* New Haven, 1980, Cat. 43, repr.

REFERENCES: Pavière (96), repr. in col. pl.2; D'Oench, list 132, and Cat. 43, repr.; A Local Conversation Piece, *Bradford Antiquary,* March 1939, pp.397–402, repr. p.398; Ellis Waterhouse, English Conversation Pieces of the Eighteenth Century, *Burlington Magazine* 88, June, 1946, p.151, repr. pl.153B; Sitwell, The World of Arthur Devis, *The Saturday Book* 12, 1952, p.92; Retratos Ingleses en la Real Academia de Londres, *Goya* 18, May-June 1957, p.364, repr. p.360; Mario Praz, *Conservation Pieces: A Survey of the Informal Group Portrait in Europe and America,* Pennsylvania, 1971, p.143, repr. pl.292; Robert Gibson and Keith Roberts, *British Portrait Painters,* London, 1971, repr. pl.19; William Gaunt, *The Great Century of British Painting: Hogarth to Turner,* Oxford, 1978, repr. pl.48, 49; Aileen Ribeiro, 18th Century English Costume, *Antique Collector,* Feb. 1978, repr. in det. p.93.

52. Nicholas Fazackerley, M.P., Recorder of Preston, Lancashire   1763   P

Signature and date no longer visible
Canvas, 92 × 58 in.
Harris Museum and Art Gallery, Preston

Nicholas Fazackerley was the leading politician associated with Preston in the eighteenth century. He succeeded Daniel Pulteney as member of Parliament for the town in 1732, and ten years later was also appointed Recorder of Preston. Both of these offices he held until his death in 1767.

This powerful and articulate lawyer actively pursued the interests of the Tory party at Westminster, voting against the Walpole Administration in every recorded division of its reign.[1] Though described by Horace Walpole as "a tiresome Jacobite lawyer," his vocation made him sufficiently cautious never to allow himself to be accused of betraying English interests. Nevertheless, he was always present to oppose the Hanoverian cause where and when the situation was opportune. Similarly in Preston he vigorously espoused Tory principles, and was responsible for organising the town's government which so effectively excluded the Whigs from any real power until the General Election of 1768.

This full-length portrait, unique in scale and handling in Devis' oeuvre, was presented to Preston Corporation as the result of a bequest by the barrister, Robert Boulton. Evidently inspired by a high regard for his former tutor, by a will dated circa 1759 he made the bequest in the following words — "I give to my good and worthy master, Nicholas Fazackerley, Esq., if he be living at the time of my decease (but not otherwise) the sum of Fifty Pounds, with which I desire he will make a present of his picture to the Corporation of Preston, in order to be set up in the Town Hall of the said borough as a memorandum that the said Corporation had once an honest man to represent them in Parliament."

The portrait, said by Pavière[2] to have been signed, Art Devis pinx.1763, (though no trace of the signature can now be found), has always been given as by Anthony Devis in early histories of the town. However, apart from the fact that it is entirely uncharacteristic of Arthur's half-brother, who was a landscape painter, there can be no doubt as to its authenticity. It was in the exhibition of the Free Society in 1770, where it was catalogued as *No 62 A gentleman – whole length.* A catalogue annotated in Horace Walpole's hand[3] appends the name Mr. Fazackerley to the entry.

Almost certainly, Devis adopted the stance of Nicholas Fazackerley in the composition in order for it to be a pendant to a similar large-scale portrait of Daniel Pulteney, M.P., which dates from about 1730 and was at the time hanging in the Town Hall. There is no evidence to suggest that the interior depicted by Devis is based on Preston Town Hall itself.

1. Romney Sedgwick, *The History of Parliament, The House of Commons, 1715–54* (H.M.S.O. London 1970), vol.2, pp.27–28.

2. See Pavière (40).

3. See Notes by Horace Walpole, fourth Earl of Orford on the Exhibitions of the Society of Artists and the Free Society of Artists, 1760–1791, Ed. Hugh Gatty, *Walpole Society*, 1938–39, p.64.

PROVENANCE: Preston Town Hall; now in the Harris Museum and Art Gallery.

EXHIBITED: Free Society of Artists, 1770.

REFERENCES: Pavière (40); D'Oench, list 60; William Dobson, *History of the Parliamentary Representation of Preston during the last Hundred Years*, Preston, 1868, pp.31–33.

53. Portrait of Samuel Richardson 1750
Joseph Highmore   (1692–1780)   P
Signed and dated
Canvas, 20¾ × 14½ in.
National Portrait Gallery, London

Samuel Richardson,[1] author of *Clarissa* and *Pamela*, takes up a formal stance with his hand tucked in his waistcoat. In describing a similar costume to the one he is wearing, another great novelist, Sir Walter Scott, suggested that "who, meaning the costume of his hero to be impressive, would willingly attire him in the court dress of George the Second's reign, with its no collar, large sleeves, and low pocket holes?"[2]

Highmore's brushwork has a bravura which enables him to capture a spontaneity of gesture and to convey an insight into the character of his sitter not possessed by Devis. However, in doing so he loses the carefully-wrought naivety which is such an intrinsic aspect of all the works of Devis.

This work is also interesting for its depiction of the painting over the mantelpiece, which is a version of the following catalogue entry.

1. For full information on this painting see John Kerslake, *Early Georgian Portraits*, vol.1, p.232 et seq.

2. See Walter Scott, *Waverley Novels*, Edinburgh, Robert Cadell, 1842, Chap.1, p.46.

PROVENANCE: Lady Bradshaigh; her sister, Elizabeth Bellingham (d. 1783), married Sir Robert Echlin, 2nd Bt.; the portrait is likely to have passed through their daughter, Elizabeth, wife of Francis Palmer of Swords, Co. Dublin, to Emma, daughter and sole heir of Joseph Hudworth Palmer, who married in 1812 W. A. MacKinnon, 33rd Chief; his son, W. A. MacKinnon, of Hyde Park Place and Acryse Park, Kent; sold from his collection, Robinson and Fisher, Oct. 31, 1895, Lot 31, bt. Colnaghi's; bt. by the National Portrait Gallery, 1896.

EXHIBITED: Moscow and Leningrad, British Council Exhibition, *British Painting, 1700–1960* (2).

REFERENCES: John Kerslake, see note 1.

54. Sir Roger and Lady Bradshaigh, of Haigh Hall, Lancashire 1746
Edward Haytley   (fl. c. 1740–65)   P
Inscribed with the names of the sitters and the artist, with the date
Canvas, 26½ × 34 in.
Metropolitan Borough of Wigan

This is one of the finest examples of the work of Edward Haytley, whose paintings have often been confused with those of Arthur Devis. There can be no doubt that the artists must have known each other; both of them apparently worked for the same patrons.[1]

A comparison of this painting with the conversation pieces of Devis reveals a similar carefully-wrought craftmanship, with an attention to detail. The figures also are more tonally integrated with their surroundings. A feature of Haytley's painting which differentiates him from Devis is his perspective drawing which often, as in this case, gives the impression that a chair or a table is tilted towards the spectator.

The picture is important for its associations. Lady Bradshaigh was a fervent admirer of Richardson's novels. Having corresponded for some time they eventually met in Joseph Highmore's studio to see the artist's paintings of illustrations to the novel *Pamela*. In 1750 Richardson asked Lady Bradshaigh if she would allow Highmore to make a copy of this painting,[2] adding that "You know not the pleasure I shall have in looking upon it, when you are at that seat (i.e. Haigh Hall) which is there drawn in so lively a manner, and is so very delightful." In return, Lady Bradshaigh asked for a replica of Highmore's portrait of Richardson. This replica is now in the National Portrait Gallery, and is here displayed as the previous catalogue entry.

1. Both Haytley and Devis worked for the Farington family of Shawe Hall, Lancashire. See D'Oench, Cat. 9. Haytley also painted a portrait of Sir William Milner, of Nun Appleton Hall, Yorkshire, 1764, which is a pendant to a portrait by Devis of Lady Milner, 1760. See Sotheby sale catalogue, March 12, 1980, with repr. of the two pictures.

2. See John Harris, *The Artist and the Country House*, 1979, p.219, no. 236.

PROVENANCE: Probably Elizabeth Echlin, Lady Bradshaigh's sister; by descent to Emma MacKinnon, née Palmer; by descent to her great-great-grandson, the present Mackinnon of Mackinnon; Sotheby's, Nov. 12, 1980 (29); bt. Wigan Metropolitan Borough Council, for Haigh Hall, with the aid of a contribution from the N.A.C.F.

REFERENCES: N.A.C.F. Annual Report.

55. Artist's Lay-Figure, formerly owned by Louis-François Roubiliac   c. 1740
26¾ in. high
The Museum of London

It was common practice in eighteenth-century England for portrait painters to use the lay-figure[1] (or large doll) as a substitute for the sitter, who was thus saved the inconvenience of repeated visits to the studio. The degree of sophistication in their construction varied considerably, as did their price.[2] This fine lay-figure, wearing original clothes from its own wardrobe, was owned by the sculptor, Louis-François Roubiliac (1703–1762). By comparison with others manufactured at the time, it is extremely realistic. It has a body modelled in cork, covered with a fine stockinette, convincingly imitating the human form, and a carved and painted wooden head.[3] In spite of its maker's attempts to capture a true-to-life appearance, there is an awkwardness of articulation which contrasts with the natural stance of a living person. This was recognised in a letter dated October 21, 1793, from an artists' colourman, John Wragg, who had purchased the lay-figure for a Mr. Richard French –
"... as to the Shape of the figure which should have been formed, as much of Elastick Composition as possible, I found to be made of Cork, which greatly incumbers the joints (and that without the least Stay, to prevent the Substances from being Loose on the Body and turning Round on the arms and thighs, of the Skeleton) in the first place it appears, that all the Socket, Tho Exceeding good work have originally Been made so deep, that the Screws Could not draw the joints any closer, and thirdly the Swivel on which the figure turns, which should have been put, as much in the Buttox, as possible, is plac'd to the front. But this I could not alter and youl pleas Sir to observe, that the Square End of the iron, that Rises from the Stand, gos into the Socket of this Ball, and notwithstanding there is some Objections to the Elbows, and Standing of the Body joints, yet, I think the figure, will be found to be a very Useful Apparatus..." [4]

Also belonging to the lay-figure is a female wardrobe comprising a black silk hat with a pink ribbon, hair, a hooded cloak of red flannel, a cambric smock, and a holland skirt.

Another interesting costume is a military one of George II's army, which must have been used for the figure of Viscount Shannon on his monument at Walton-on-Thames. Unfortunately, it belongs to a lost, smaller lay-figure, which must also have been owned by Roubiliac.

1. Lay-figures were owned by Sir Joshua Reynolds, Thomas Gainsborough, Hubert Gravelot, and of course Arthur Devis, among others.

2. In 1770 the Incorporated Society's Academy of Drawing decided to purchase a lay-figure at a cost of not more than £20. The following year, the Royal Academy Schools purchased one for the extremely high price of "about £80." Second-hand lay-figures were surprisingly cheap. Whitley records that Gainsborough's lay-figure "most ingeniously constructed with brass-work joints," was sold by his widow for £3, while that belonging to Sir Joshua Reynolds, which he passed on to his assistant, Giuseppe Marchi, changed hands for 15s.0d.

3. The features of the head were carefully chosen to allow the figure to be used with clothes of either sex.

4. John Wragg's address was 25 Denmark Street, nr. Soho Square. He had apparently acquired the lay-figure for Richard French, to whom the letter was addressed. Little is known of Richard French, but he is mentioned in a letter dated October 13, 1791, from Erasmus Darwin to Horace Walpole, which demonstrates his interest in sculpture.

PROVENANCE: Louis-François Roubiliac, his sale, May 12–15, 1762 (88); unknown, until bt. by John Wragg, artists' colourman, for Richard French, 1793; with J. J. Linzell, c. 1928, whose grandfather had owned it; purchased by Ernest S. Makower, on behalf of the London Museum, 1929.

REFERENCES: Sale *Catalogue of the Genuine and Entire Collection of Models, Moulds, Casts and Busts ... Mr. Roubiliac's late Dwelling House, St. Martin's Lane, London, May 12–15, 1762*; Mrs. Arundell Esdaile, 'Roubiliac: Some Unrecorded Details connected with his Life and Work,' *Archaeological Journal*, LXXXVI, 1929, pp.178–186, repr. in different costumes; William T. Whitley, Artists and their Friends in England from 1700 to 1799, *Medici Society*, London, 1928, vol.1, pp.236 and 278 for information on lay-figures; D'Oench, pp.13, 14.

56. Lay-Figure Costumes, formerly owned by Arthur Devis   c. 1755
Harris Museum and Art Gallery, Preston

The lay-figure costumes were acquired by the Harris Museum and Art Gallery from Mrs. C. Tupper, a descendant of the Devis family, and in view of other items which were in her possession it is reasonable to suppose that they were owned by

Arthur Devis. The hussar suit comprising a jacket and breeches in blue silk satin trimmed with yellow braid, and pink cuffs, is sufficiently similar to costumes in two pictures, *William Henry Ricketts, and his Wife Mary, in the Grounds of Ranelagh,*[1] and *Gentleman in Hussar Costume*[2] (formerly entitled *William Henry Ricketts*), for it to have been used by Devis. Unfortunately, none of the magnificent costumes in paintings such as *Edward Parker and his Wife Barbara, of Browsholme Hall, near Clitheroe* (Cat. 42, see repr. in col.), or *Edward Rookes-Leeds and his Family, of Royds Hall, Low Moor, Yorkshire* (Cat. 51, see repr. in col.) now exist.

Other items on display include a hussar jacket in pink satin trimmed with yellow braid and edged with white fur; a waistcoat in natural off-white linen; a waistcoat-front in pale pink silk with false pocket flaps and buttonholes; a stocking knitted in white cotton; and a bodice for a female figure in blue corded silk with a laced fastening. From the size of the costumes, Devis' lay-figure must have been about 30 inches high.

The reliance placed by artists on the lay-figure varied considerably. Sometimes it served as a general aid in arranging the pose of a figure, or organising a group in a conversation piece. On other occasions it enabled the artist to complete the painting of a costume in the absence of a sitter. Devis, however, added a new dimension by exploiting the angular articulation and doll-like characteristics as an essential feature in his paintings.

1. See Sacheverell Sitwell, *Conversation Pieces*, London, 1936, repr. pl.53.

2. Repr. in sale catalogue, Sotheby's, February 24, 1960 (118).

PROVENANCE: By descent from the Devis family to Mrs. C. Tupper; purchased from her by the Harris Museum and Art Gallery, 1936.

EXHIBITED: Edinburgh, Scottish National Portrait Gallery, *Van Dyck in Check Trousers, Fancy Dress in Art and Life, 1700–1900,* 1978 (9) (Hussar Costume only); Museum of London, *Masquerade,* 1983 (Hussar Costume only).

REFERENCES: Pavière, p.30; D'Oench, p.13; Aileen Ribeiro, 'Hussars in Masquerade,' *Apollo,* Feb. 1977.

57. Margaret Ainge   c. 1768
Oil on glass, 12 × 9 in.   P
Victoria and Albert Museum, London

This portrait is one of several known to have been executed by Devis between the years 1768 and 1780. Although dated 1780, by Pavière, because of an entry *'227 A Portrait on glass'* in the catalogue of the Free Society of Artists, this can be rejected on the grounds that the hair-style is a 'Dutch Coiffure,' popular from the 1740s to the 1760s. Stylistically, and on the basis of Horace Walpole's annotation in the catalogue of the Free Society of Artists for 1768,[1] the painting may be dated about that year.

It was owned by Mrs. C. Tupper, a descendant of Devis, and from other portraits which were in her possession may well be of a relation of the artist.

Margaret Ainge (or Angier) was possibly a descendant of the Angier family, formerly of Dedham in Essex, and later of Manchester.[2]

1. See *Walpole Society*, vol.27, 1938–39, Hugh Gatty, Notes by Horace Walpole, on the exhibitions of the Society of Artists and the Free Society of Artists, 1760–1791. What Devis describes as a new species of painting is according to Walpole "I believe painted behind the glass."

2. D.N.D. See biography of John Angier (1605–77). 77).

PROVENANCE: Mrs. C. Tupper; Christie's, May 22, 1936(54); bt. Brook Street Galleries, London; Lawrence Venn, 1945; Victoria and Albert Museum.

EXHIBITED: Preston, *Lancashire Art,* 1937(20).

REFERENCES: Pavière (3); D'Oench. list 260.

58. Self-Portrait, miniature   c. 1742
Oil on copper, 1¾ × 1½ in. oval
Harris Museum and Art Gallery, Preston

Devis painted this, together with the following portrait miniature of his wife, Elizabeth Faulkner, about the year 1742. Although its small scale is unusual for Devis, it can be attributed to him stylistically and on the basis of an inscription on a backing card holding it in the frame, in the early nineteenth century hand of a member of the Tupper family, which reads *Arthur/Devis/An oil portrait/on copper/mar/17.*

PROVENANCE: By descent from the Devis family to Mrs. C. Tupper; purchased by the Harris Museum and Art Gallery, 1936.

REFERENCES: Pavière, pp.30, 31; D'Oench, list 48.

59. Elizabeth Faulkner, Wife of Arthur Devis, miniature   c. 1742

Oil on copper, 1¾ × 1½ in. oval
Harris Museum and Art Gallery, Preston

Pendant to Cat. 58. Inscribed on a backing card in the hand of a member of the Tupper family — *Elizabeth/Faulkner/(Mrs. Arthur Devis)/an oil portrait/on copper/mar./17.*

PROVENANCE: By descent from the Devis family to Mrs. C. Tupper; purchased by the Harris Museum and Art Gallery, 1936.

REFERENCES: Pavière, pp.30, 31; D'Oench, list 51.

60. Elizabeth Faulkner, Wife of Arthur Devis c. 1742   P

Oil on panel, 7½ × 6½ in.
Harris Museum and Art Gallery, Preston

Elizabeth Faulkner married Arthur Devis on July 20, 1742. This portrait shows her seated at a table, holding a mirror (as a symbol of her own beauty) and a locket of a young man, presumably Arthur Devis. It is reasonable to assume that the portrait was painted shortly after the marriage. The date is also confirmed by the style of the costume.

Interestingly, the table in the portrait was added later, and saponification of the oil paint shows the costume underneath. Also, the hand which originally rested on her lap was re-painted to hold the mirror.

The painting is inscribed on the reverse *Mrs. Devis, the Mother of M (?) Devis Devonshire Place.* Also in the same hand — *This picture to be sent to Miss El. Devis No. 20 Devonshire Place.* In another hand, identified as that of a member of the Tupper family (See Cat. 58), is inscribed *formerly Elizabeth Faulkner.*

The Miss El. Devis referred to in the inscription is Miss Ellin Devis, daughter of Arthur Devis, who lived for many years at 20 Devonshire Place, Marylebone, London, and who died Feb. 21, 1820. Possibly the portrait was sent to Miss Devis on the death of her mother in 1788.

PROVENANCE: Miss Ellin Devis; by descent to the Tupper family; purchased, 1980, by the Harris

Museum and Art Gallery, with the aid of a grant from the N.A.C.F., from Miss Elizabeth Lee of Iver, Buckinghamshire, whose father acquired it c. 1935.

REFERENCES: N.A.C.F. Annual Report.

61. Arthur Devis 1787
Anthony Devis (1729–1816)   P

Pencil, 6¼ × 5⅛ in. oval
Harris Museum and Art Gallery, Preston

This profile portrait of Arthur Devis in the year of his death was drawn by his half-brother, Anthony (See Cat. 64). It represents an unusual departure for Anthony, who is exclusively known for his landscape paintings, in particular his topographical and picturesque watercolours.

The drawing is inscribed within an oval shape *ARTHUR DEVIS 1787* and *Anth. Devis Delin.* There is another inscription in the hand of a member of the Tupper family, which reads *Isabelle's grandfather.*

PROVENANCE: By descent from the Devis family to Mrs. C. Tupper; purchased by the Harris Museum and Art Gallery, 1936.

62. Elizabeth Faulkner, Wife of Arthur Devis,   c. 1780–83
Arthur William Devis (1762–1822)   P

Pencil and watercolour, 7¾ × 5⅞ in. oval
Harris Museum and Art Gallery, Preston

Arthur William, son of Arthur Devis, received his initial art training from his father, and entered the Royal Academy Schools at the age of 12 years. There he is said to have won a silver medal for his draftsmanship, and to have been praised by Sir Joshua Reynolds, who was President at the time.

This pencil and watercolour drawing of his mother was executed some time before 1783, when he was appointed draftsman to the East India Company vessel, 'Antelope', and set sail on a voyage around the world. He was shipwrecked on the Pelew Islands, and subsequently visited Canton and India, where he obtained many portrait commissions. By the time he returned home in 1795, both his parents were dead.

The drawing is inscribed, in the hand of a member of the Tupper family, *Elizabeth (Faulkner) wife of Arthur Devis.*

PROVENANCE: Unknown, but from the inscription must have been in the Tupper family, who obtained it by descent from the Devis family; probably bought by the Harris Museum and Art Gallery from Mrs. C. Tupper, 1936.

63. Anthony, Father of Arthur Devis
c. 1742

Oil on double thickness of canvas, 3³/₈ × 2⁷/₈ in.
oval
Harris Museum and Art Gallery, Preston

This is the only known portrait of Arthur Devis' father, Anthony (born c. 1688). It has been laid down on another piece of canvas, which had been part of an unfinished conversation piece. This portion comprises an arm and dress of a seated woman.

There is an inscription on a backing card, in the hand of a member of the Tupper family, which reads *Anthony Devis/who married Ann/Blackburne.* Ann Blackburne was the second wife of Anthony Devis, and step-mother to Arthur.

PROVENANCE: Miss Ellin Devis; by descent to the Tupper family; purchased, 1980, by the Harris Museum and Art Gallery from Mrs. C. Skinner, Stoke Poges, Buckinghamshire, with the aid of a grant from the N.A.C.F.

REFERENCES: N.A.C.F. Annual Report.

64. Anthony, Half-Brother of Arthur Devis
c. 1742

Oil on a double thickness of canvas, 3¹/₄ × 2³/₄ in.
oval
Harris Museum and Art Gallery, Preston

Anthony Devis (1729–1816) was a half-brother to Arthur, and was himself a topographical painter, principally in watercolours.

On a backing card is inscribed in the hand of a member of the Tupper family *Anthony/(John crossed out) Devis/1st (2nd crossed out) son of/ Anthony Devis/&/Ann Blackburn.*

Another portrait of Anthony Devis, similarly oval-shaped and measuring 4⁷/₈ × 3³/₄ in., was in the Mrs. C. Tupper sale at Christie's, May 22, 1936, wrongly catalogued as Arthur William Devis. It is now in a private collection, London. See D'Oench, list 46.

PROVENANCE: Miss Ellin Devis; by descent to the Tupper family; purchased, 1980, by the Harris Museum and Art Gallery from Mrs. C. Skinner, Stoke Poges, Buckinghamshire, with the aid of a grant from the N.A.C.F.

REFERENCES: N.A.C.F. Annual Report.

65. John, Half-Brother of Arthur Devis
c. 1742

Oil on double thickness of canvas, 3³/₈ × 2³/₄ in.
oval
Harris Museum and Art Gallery, Preston

John Devis was a brother of Anthony (See Cat. 64) and a half-brother of Arthur. He lived with his brother, Anthony, in London for many years, and was a watchmaker. It is the only known portrait of John, and was painted at the same time as Cat. 63 and 64.

As with Cat. 63, *Anthony, Father of Arthur Devis,* the portrait has been laid down on a piece of canvas which has been part of an unfinished conversation piece, comprising the lower half of a standing man.

It is inscribed on a backing card, in the hand of a member of the Tupper family, *John Devis/2nd son of/Anthony Devis/&/Miss Blackburn.*

PROVENANCE: Miss Ellin Devis; by descent to the Tupper family; purchased, 1980, by the Harris Museum and Art Gallery from Mrs. C. Skinner, Stoke Poges, Buckinghamshire, with the aid of a grant from the N.A.C.F.

REFERENCES: N.A.C.F. Annual Report.

66. Double Portrait Miniature of Prince Charles Edward and Arthur Devis
c. 1746–80
Unknown artist

Oil on ivory, 2¹/₂ × 1³/₄ in., portraits in ovals measuring 2 × 1³/₄ in., the whole enclosed in glass, 3⁷/₈ × 1¹/₈ in.
Harris Museum and Art Gallery, Preston

This double portrait miniature of Prince Charles Edward, the Young Pretender (verso), and Arthur Devis (recto), illustrates a legend that the two very closely resembled each other. A manuscript account written by Ellin Isabelle Tupper[1] in 1895 describes an anecdote handed down by family tradition that "As a young man, Mr. Devis was considered so like Charles Edward (commonly known as the Young Pretender) that he was upon one occasion arrested and only not killed on the spot because the soldiers thought they would get a better reward if they took him alive. A slight hesitation of speech made them sure their captive was guilty, but fortunately friends came up and he was released; but it was not considered safe for him to remain in Preston, Lancashire, after that, so he left his father's house and repaired to London, then a week's journey." Pavière rightly points out that by the time the incident is said to have taken place, Anthony Devis, Arthur's father, had already removed to London. On the other hand the family must have retained close ties with Preston, for Bartholomew, Arthur's brother, who was a watchmaker in London in 1742, was apparently living in Preston in 1758.[2]

Devis is also recorded in Matthew Pilkington's *Dictionary of Painters*, 1824, as having "so strong a resemblance to the Pretender, that in this period of political ferment, he was obliged to quit Preston incognito." This is probably the source used by Martin Tupper for his play *The Pretender and his Double*,[3] which romanticises the event.

The double portrait consists of a piece of ivory, on one side of which is a supposed portrait of Prince Charles Edward, below which is inscribed *The Young Pretender/Charles Edward Stuart/in 1746.[4]/Derby*, and on the other an image in reverse, said to be Arthur Devis, with the inscription *His Double,/Arthur Devis;/of Preston./1746*. It appears to have been made by drawing one of the portraits, and then tracing it through the thin ivory onto the opposite side. The better of the two, that of Prince Charles Edward, is a free version of the glamourised portraits of the Prince, popularised in mid-eighteenth century enamels. The portrait of Devis is coarser in drawing and handling of paint, and is almost certainly the one which was traced. Devis' authorship is difficult to sustain, on the grounds that it is not sufficiently well executed, and that it is a deception based on an imaginary portrait of Prince Charles Edward, and quite unlike himself. Devis' two sons, Thomas Anthony (1757–1810) and Arthur William (1762–1822), were portrait painters, and Anthony Devis (1729–1816), his half-brother, although a landscape painter, executed the drawing of Arthur Devis in 1787 (Cat. 61). It is possible that one of them painted the miniature at an early age. There is also the question raised by the inscriptions which are the only means of identifying the portraits. They are written in the same nineteenth-century hand which has inscribed other portraits formerly in the possession of the Tupper family (Cat. 58–65).

A comparison of the self-portraits of Devis (Cat. 1, 2, 33, and 58) with authentic portraits of Prince Charles Edward does, however, show a similarity of features which may have been even more pronounced in the flesh if the artist admired the Prince sufficiently to imitate his mannerisms. This, together with the known Jacobite sympathies of a significant number of Devis' patrons, suggests that there may be some truth in the legend.

1. Ellin Isabelle Tupper was a descendant of Martin Farquhar Tupper (1810–89), a prolific writer remembered for his *Proverbial Philosophy*, 1838–42, a collection of commonplace maxims in verse. He was a great-grandson of Devis, and son-in-law of Arthur William Devis (Cat. 62). The Tupper family acquired many personal effects of the Devis family through Devis' daughter, Ellin, who died unmarried in 1820, leaving her estate to her niece, Ellin Devis Marris, mother of Martin Tupper.

2. He was elected a Bailiff of Preston in 1758. In later years he was elected Councillor (1763), Alderman (1773), and Mayor (1774, 1780, and 1785).

3. See note 1. The play was included in *Three Five-Act Plays and Twelve Dramatic Scenes*, London, 1882.

4. The inscription cannot be correct. Prince Charles Edward and his army retreated northwards from Derby on December 6, 1745.

PROVENANCE: By descent from the Devis family to Mrs. C. Tupper; purchased from her by the Harris Museum and Art Gallery, 1936.

REFERENCES: Pavière, pp.29, 30, repr. pl.6; D'Oench, list 196.

67. Model Tomb   c. 1788

16¾ × 13½ in., 9½ in. in depth   P
Harris Museum and Art Gallery, Preston

Arthur Devis died at Brighton on July 25, 1787. His wife, Elizabeth, died eight months later on March 15, 1788. Both were buried "under a plain stone" in St. Mary's churchyard, Paddington Green, London.

This model tomb to their memory was commissioned by their daughter, Ellin, "the mistress of a highly respectable seminary for young ladies of fashion."[1] It comprises a pedestal surmounted by an urn in imitation of a tomb, the whole enclosed in a cabinet with a glazed window with satinwood tracery. The window was based on the architecture of the long-demolished church of St. Katherine in the Tower, where they were married on July 20, 1742. The urn contains the hair of the couple, together with Mrs. Devis' wedding ring. In the lid of the urn is a representation of a weeping willow with sixteen branches chopped off and six remaining. This is in remembrance of the twenty-two children of the marriage, only six of whom survived.

Inside the pedestal are two miniatures of Arthur Devis (2 × 2¼ in.) and his wife (1¾ × 2⅛ in.) taken after death by Richard Corbould[2] (1751–1831). On that of Arthur are the words:—
Behold the virtuous man in his last moments
Calm and serene he yields his latest breath
And may be said to triumph over death.

and on the miniature of his wife is a quotation from Proverbs XXVII, 1:—

> Boast not thyself of tomorrow — for thou Knowest not what a day may bring forth.

On an ivory disc set in the front of the tomb is an inscription, *Arthur Devis, born at Preston in Lancashire on the 19th Febry. 1711[3] and died at Brighthelmstone in Sussex at 4 o'clock in the afternoon on Wednesday the 25th July 1787 in the 77th year of his age.* On the back is a further inscription, *In memory of an invaluable Parent and Friend in whom every Virtue that could adorn a human character was united. This little tribute is offered by a daughter who tho' taught by Reason and Religion to bear, yet must ever feel her afflictive loss, for in the sweet society of her Father she not only felt all the comfort that paternal tenderness could afford, but unitedly all the delights of the most pure friendship. May the constant remembrance of his affection have a proper effect on her mind and may his descendants to the latest generations endeavour to emulate his exemplary life.*[1]

On the sides of the tomb are two allegorical paintings described by Ellin Isabelle Tupper[4] as *Time perceiving the Hourglass of Life to be exhausted is extinguishing an almost expiring flame,* and *Virtue rewarding the honourable Industry of age is pointing out the glories which await him in a brighter region.*

The evidence of the inscriptions on the tomb suggests that the model was originally commissioned in memory of Arthur Devis shortly after his death, and that it was altered to accommodate the miniature, hair and ring of Mrs. Devis, following her death shortly afterwards.

1. Edward Edwards, *Anecdotes of Painters who have resided or been born in England,* 1808, p.123. Edwards also refers to a short grammar of the English language which Miss Devis had published "for the use of the younger part of her own sex; which has been much approved."

2. Richard Corbould was a pupil of Robert Marris, who married Frances, the second surviving daughter of Devis. He was not only a painter in oil and watercolours, but also a painter of miniatures on porcelain and ivory, and in enamel. He is also remembered as a book illustrator.

3. 1711 O.S., 1712 N.S.

4. Ellin Isabelle Tupper compiled a short MS account of the Devis family in 1895. This is now in the Harris Museum and Art Gallery.

PROVENANCE: By descent from the Devis family to Mrs. C. Tupper; purchased by the Harris Museum and Art Gallery, 1936.

REFERENCES: Pavière, pp.30, 31.

Illustrations

2. Self-Portrait
1742
Harris Museum and Art Gallery, Preston

4. **Peter Tillemans (c. 1684–1734)**
   Uppark, West Sussex, c. 1725
   Private Collection

Far Left
5. John Orlebar, of Hinwick House, Bedfordshire
   c. 1740
   Private Collection

Left
6. John Orlebar, of Hinwick House, Bedfordshire
   c. 1740
   Harris Museum and Art Gallery, Preston

7. The Rev. William Farington, of Leigh, Lancashire
   c. 1741–42
   Harris Museum and Art Gallery, Preston

8. Ralph Assheton, of Cuerdale Hall, near Preston, Lancashire
   1742
   Private Collection

11. Roger Hesketh and his Family, of Rossall, Lancashire
    c. 1742–43
    Roger Fleetwood Hesketh, Lancashire

12. Children in an Interior
    c. 1742—43
    Yale Center for British Art, Paul Mellon Collection, New Haven, Connecticut, U.S.A.

13. Robert Gwillym of Atherton, and his Family
     c. 1745–46
     Yale Center for British Art, Paul Mellon Collection, New Haven, Connecticut, U.S.A.

14. William Atherton and his Wife, Lucy, of Preston, Lancashire
    c. 1742—44
    Walker Art Gallery, Liverpool

16. Gentleman and Lady in a Landscape
    c. 1747–49
    The National Trust, Wimpole Hall, Arrington, Cambridgeshire

17. The Duet
1749
Victoria and Albert Museum

18. Robert Dashwood and his Wife, Anne, of Stamford Park, Nottinghamshire
1750
Private Collection

19. Louis Combrune, of Lothbury
    1745
    Private Collection

20. Wrightson Mundy, of Osbaston, Leicestershire, and Markeaton,
    Derbyshire
    1749
    Private Collection

21. Thomas Starkie, of Frenchwood House, Preston
1749
Harris Museum and Art Gallery, Preston

22. Miss Sarah Tyssen, of Hackney, Middlesex
1748
Private Collection

23. Lady in a Blue Dress
    c. 1748
    Private Collection

3 Hoghton Tower from Duxon Hill, Lancashire.
1735.

9 Breaking-up Day at John Clayton's School in Salford.
c. 1738–40.

10 John Bacon and his Family
   c. 1742—43

15 The Rev. Streynsham Master and his Wife, of Croston, Lancashire.
    1742–44.

40 Henry Fiennes Clinton, ninth Earl of Lincoln, with his Wife, Catherine, and Son, George.
   c. 1751

42 Edward Parker and his Wife, Barbara, on the Terrace at Browsholme Hall, near Clitheroe.
1757

48 Richard Lowe, of Denby and Locko Park, Derbyshire.
c. 1761–2

51 Edward Rookes-Leeds and his Family, of Royds Hall, Low Moor, Yorkshire.
    c. 1763-68

24. Lucy Watson (later Mrs. John Thornton of Clapham)
c. 1749
Trustees of R. J. Meade-Fetherstonhaugh, decd., on loan to Uppark, West Sussex

97

25. Sir James Burrow, of Starborough Castle, Lingfield, Surrey
1749
Private Collection

26. William Wallis Lethieullier (called Boy Fishing)
c. 1749
Trustees of R. J. Meade-Fetherstonhaugh,
decd., on loan to Uppark, West Sussex

98

27. Mr. and Mrs. Van Harthals with their Son
1749
The National Trust, Bearsted Collection, Upton House, Warwickshire

Above
31. The Boldero Brothers, of Cornborough, Yorkshire
    1752
    Yale University Art Gallery, Bequest of Helen Huntington Hull

Right
33. Self-Portrait
    c. 1754
    Harris Museum and Art Gallery, Preston

Right
32 Gentleman at a Sundial
    c. 1755
    Private Collection

Below
34. Assheton Curzon, later Viscount Curzon, of Penn House,
     Buckinghamshire, with his Tutor, Dr. Mather
     c. 1754
     Private Collection

Below Right
35. John Lockwood, of Dews Hall, Essex
     c. 1757
     Simon Cotton, Hertfordshire

Far Right
36. Mrs. John Lockwood, (née Matilda Conyers), of Dews Hall,
     Essex   c. 1757
     Simon Cotton, Hertfordshire

Above
37. John, second Lord Monson, with his eldest Son, John, in Broxbournebury Park,
Herefordshire
c. 1756
Mrs. William Dalison Keown-Boyd, on loan to the Harris Museum and Art Gallery,
Preston

Right
38. Sir Roger Newdigate in his Library at Arbury Hall, Warwickshire
c. 1756–58
Trustees of the Newdigate Settlement

106

41. Edward Gordon, his Sister, Mrs. Miles, and Her Husband, in their Garden at Bromley,
Kent
1756
Leicestershire Museums and Art Galleries, Leicester

44. Col. John Sabine, and his Family, in the Park at Tewin House, Hertfordshire
    c. 1758
    Private Collection

111

Above
49. Elizabeth and Charlotte Edgar, of Red House Park,
Ipswich, Suffolk
1762
The National Trust, Bearsted Collection, Upton House,
Warwickshire

Right
50. Francis Vincent, his Wife Mercy, and Daughter Ann,
of Weddington Hall, Warwickshire
1763
Harris Museum and Art Gallery, Preston

Far Right
52. Nicholas Fazackerley, M.P., Recorder of Preston, Lancashire
1763
Harris Museum and Art Gallery, Preston

Right
53. **Joseph Highmore (1692–1780)**
Portrait of Samuel Richardson, 1750
National Portrait Gallery

Far Right
54. **Edward Haytley (fl. c. 1740–65)**
Sir Roger and Lady Bradshaigh, of Haigh Hall,
Lancashire, 1746
Metropolitan Borough of Wigan

Below Right
58. Self-Portrait, miniature
c. 1742
Harris Museum and Art Gallery, Preston

Below Far Right
59. Elizabeth Faulkner, Wife of Arthur Devls, miniature
c. 1742
Harris Museum and Art Gallery, Preston

ger & Lady Bradshaigh   Hoadly Pinx.[superscript t]

61. **Anthony Devis (1729–1816)**
   Arthur Devis, 1787
   Harris Museum and Art Gallery, Preston

62. **Arthur William Devis (1762–1822)**
   Elizabeth Faulkner, Wife of Arthur Devis, c. 1780–83
   Harris Museum and Art Gallery, Preston

Left
63. Anthony, Father of Arthur Devis
    c. 1742
    Harris Museum and Art Gallery, Preston

Above Left
64. Anthony, Half-Brother of Arthur Devis
    c. 1742
    Harris Museum and Art Gallery, Preston

Above
65. John, Half-Brother of Arthur Devis
    c. 1742
    Harris Museum and Art Gallery, Preston

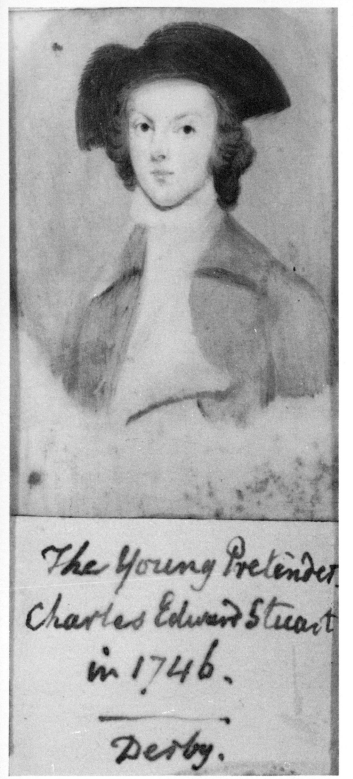

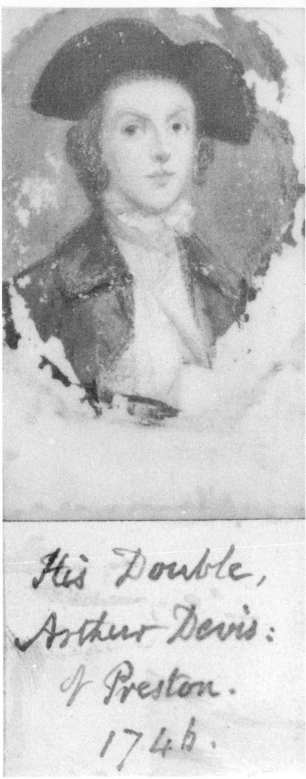

66a. Double Portrait Miniature, Prince Charles Edward c. 1746–80
Harris Museum and Art Gallery, Preston

66b. Double Portrait Miniature, Arthur Devis c. 1746–80
Harris Museum and Art Gallery, Preston